...And You Think You've Got It Bad

Turn-of-the-Century Life & House-keeping

Compiled by

Barbara Fairchild Gramm

Barbara Fairchild Gram

PIG'S EYE PRESS

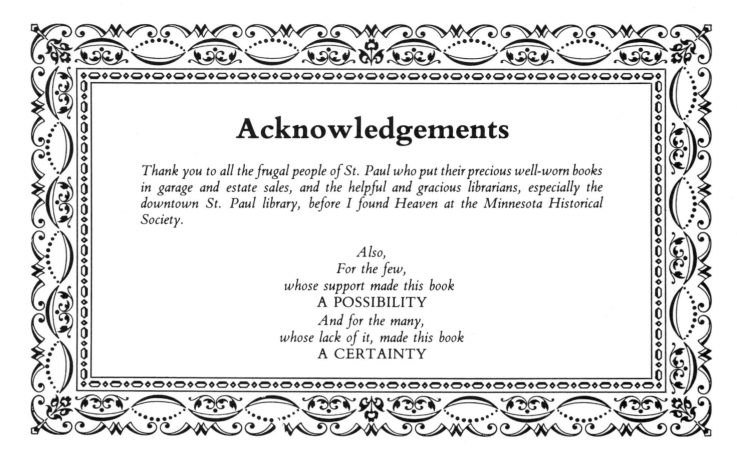

Acknowledgements

Thank you to all the frugal people of St. Paul who put their precious well-worn books in garage and estate sales, and the helpful and gracious librarians, especially the downtown St. Paul library, before I found Heaven at the Minnesota Historical Society.

Also,
For the few,
whose support made this book
A POSSIBILITY
And for the many,
whose lack of it, made this book
A CERTAINTY

Library of Congress Cataloging-in-Publication Data

Gramm, Barbara Fairchild.
    --and you think you've got it bad : turn-of-the-century life & housekeeping / by Barbara Fairchild Gramm.
      p. 144 cm. 28
    Includes bibliographical references.
    ISBN 0-9643368-0-4 $14.95
    1. Home economics--United States--History--19th century.
    2. United States--Social life and customs--19th century. I. Title.
TX153.G73 1989
640'.973'09034--dc20   89-28134
                                           CIP

Cover art: Mark Coyle

ISBN: 0-9643368-0-4

Published by:

Pig's Eye Press
152 Duke St.
St. Paul, MN 55102

Dedication

To my Family:
Myrtle Fairchild
Milton Gramm
Dave St. Martin
Steve & Nancy St. Martin
Sue & Gino Rodriguez
especially
my Precious
Grandchildren
Matthew St. Martin &
Nicole Rodriguez

To Select Well Among Old Things
Is Almost Equal to Inventing
New Ones　　TRUBLET

Contents

Introduction

At least twenty-five years ago I discovered a coverless turn-of-the-century book on housekeeping in an attic trunk which had been left by a former resident. The humor it provides today, although serious at the time it was written, led me to haunt old bookstores, garage and estate sales for material from more old, yellowed, and crumpled books. Then I began piecing together the treasures I discovered, which led to visits to library back rooms to round out what I had stumbled upon. This hobby led to the accumulation of an incredible wealth of humorous, curious, provocative, and enormously entertaining tidbits. What I have found to be the most interesting material focuses upon the role of the woman in the home and her position in society.

My discoveries have been woven into one paragraph from two or more books, altered, shortened, or simply left as is. In order to keep myself out of trouble, I decided to use only books that are in the public domain, having my references searched for copyright with the Library of Congress. After completing my work, the idea of illustrating it was born. Again, I limited my effort to those illustrations from books also in the public domain.

. . . *And You Think You've Got It Bad* is a journey back in time to the turn of the century when woman's work was menial, backbreakingly physical, and where economic and social life differed greatly from our present fast-paced, convenience-filled way of life. The seriousness of the past and its contrast with life today, particularly from the standpoint of the role of woman, has now become not only quaint, but downright hilarious.

Housework especially has remained woman's work, with comparatively little help from men, despite the fact that over half of today's married women work outside the home. The quaintness of yesterday is delightfully spiced with the laughter that the "old ways" bring to us today. Some examples:

> Do not upset your household by cleaning it all at once, as it will drive your husband to distraction and the children to the neighbors. Use a little womanly tact and clean one or two rooms at a time. When cleaning a papered wall, cut a large loaf of two-day old bread into eight pieces, blow the dust off the wall with a bellows, and rub down a piece of the bread in half-yard strokes. When washing windows, clean the corners easily by using a sharp-pointed stick such as the wings of turkeys, geese, or chickens, but don't leave them where the cat can chew them.

Or, picture, if you may, the charming sight of a pretty woman "caressing" a piece of asparagus. Or finding that your luncheon table holds white bread sandwiches holding tender young nasturtium leaves between their buttered folds.

While much of . . . *And You Think You've Got It Bad* is hopelessly antiquated and is ridiculously humorous, here and there the wisdom of the ages shines through and is just as appropriate today as it was in the last century:

> Well-dressed, well-bred, well-carriaged, is ticket enough to pass us readily through every door. But run into Heaven barefooted and bareheaded rather than miss it on account of anything in the world.

> The mother who worries should fight this bad habit as though it was a physical enemy. Bear the troubles of the day bravely and do not borrow those of tomorrow. In climbing a mountain we sometimes come to what looks like a wall of rock. Look closer and we see a narrow path to see us to safety. Always look for a path; there is always a way.

. . . *And You Think You've Got It Bad*, is light, funny, nostalgic, sentimental, revealing, and sometimes inspiring, but most of all, entertaining. It is a book that can be read at one's leisure, enjoyed one paragraph at a time, a joyful respite to the pressures and intensity of life in the 1990s.

At the turn of the century, life was extremely involved with accomplishing the many tasks and customs of the day. I've given a hint of it here. The recipes and medical advice are NOT recommended, but are included for the purpose of contrasting that era's methods—sometimes primitive, long and tedious—with those of today. Rather than inundate, many subjects have been shortened to give the general idea, laced with humor. The spellings, such as "table-spoonful" and "bedroom," and the colloquialisms, as "pease" for "peas," have been left in as much as possible to preserve the flavor of those times.

...And You Think
You've Got It Bad

"A Woman's Reason—Because It Is So"
16th Century

What Is a Woman?

A Sacred and Delicate Gift

For all those wondering just what and who is a woman, there is a very easy answer: She is direct from God, a sacred and delicate gift, with affections so great nothing short of the Infinite God can tell their bound. She is a straight and elegant figure with a wealth of hair and a clear bell-like voice, who is fashioned to refine, soothe, lift and irradiate home, society and the world. A high-bred lady is kind, courteous, thoughtful to others, and demonstrates in all her actions she is: every inch a lady!

There was a time when it was thought that no woman could sharpen a pencil, tie a parcel or sing bass. She now rows, fishes, shoots and wears her brother's outing cap. She is far more independent than her mother, she even hangs on to the strap on the street-car and gets jostled and pushed about in the crowd.

Women laugh when they can and weep when they will. Tears are useless anyway; all they contain is a little phosphate of lime, and some chlorate of sodium and water.

A woman whose hands are busy is sure to have a busier mind. The mind must work, and, if it does not find employment for the hands, it will for the tongue. Maybe she ought to take to a book and give her tongue a vacation.

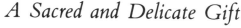

MISS SIMPLICITY'S
LECTURE
ON
Beauty Unadorned,
AT
FASHION HALL.

Ladies' Queen Fob Chains

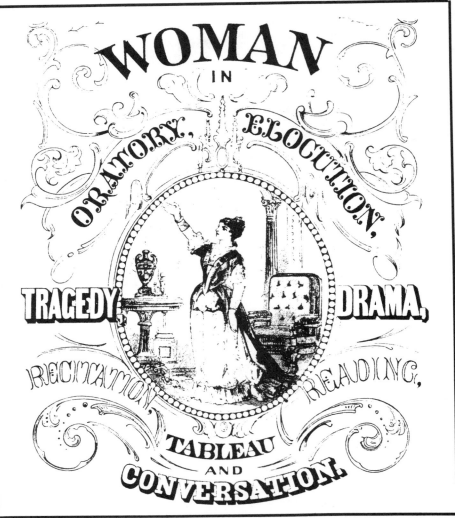

The very latest style watch chain for ladies, made of the best gold plate.

No. 1. Given for only 15 yearly subscribers, or for only 10 subscribers and 50 cents extra, or for only 6 subscribers and $1.00 extra.

It makes a very handsome present, plain polished, rolled gold plate, Roman or Etruscan finish ball charm. Sold by all jewelers for $2.50. Our price is but $1.75.

No. 2. Given for only 18 yearly subscribers, or for only 10 subscribers and 75 cents extra, or for only 8 subscribers and $1.00 extra.

An elegant rope pattern chain, Roman or Etruscan gold trimmed charm. Sold by jewelers for $3.00. Our price is but $2.00.

No. 3. Given for only 15 yearly subscribers, or for only 10 subscribers and 50 cents extra, or for only 6 subscribers and $1.00 extra.

A cable pattern chain, Roman or Etruscan gold finished charm in the shape of a very unique smelling bottle. Regular price at jewelry stores $2.50. Our price is but $1.80.

Gloves are a very essential part of a woman's attire—correct style is just as necessary in gloves as other things. The particular woman can make her selection here from the season's best styles and from superlative qualities.

Our Great Special— 16-button length mousquetaire kid gloves, with 3 pearl clasp fasteners—white only—our regular $3.00 gloves, for **$2.50**

12-button length 3 pearl clasp fasteners, white only—per pair

$2.25

Fisk 1-clasp cheverette gloves, colors tans, gun metal, black—perfect fitting—retain their shape and resist wear longer than any other glove made—per pair **$2.00**

$1.25 Princess Slips at 73c

Muslin Underwear Dept., Second Floor.

You will want two or three of these to wear with your summer dresses. They are made of good quality nainsook and trimmed with lace —special while the lot lasts, 73c each.

A Man, by Comparison

Because of the greater width of a man's head, he has greater mental powers. Women, have such a narrow brain.

As a man, even one with muttonchop whiskers, has predominance of intellect and concentration of mind he is liable to abstractness of thought and, therefore, forgets to eat, and frequently does not hear or heed the call to dinner.

A man has vigor and strength with broad shoulders and chest. He leads a life of great activity and exercise. He must be careful not to be harsh, coarse or vulgar. Due to his superior intellect, will and energy, he is the head of the household.

As a man is vastly superior in authority to the wife; she should hold him in the highest and purest regard. Without a man's restraint a family is like a horse without a driver, a nation without a ruler, a day without sun. He is as necessary as a table in a kitchen, or chairs in the parlour.

A man must understand how to steer and balance the matrimonial ship. He must use skill and judgement, patience and common sense. Common sense is quoted at a discount.

There is no motive which justifies a husband to neglect his wife, the plea of doing business or for the sake of doing good.

Her Bark Is Worse Than Her Bite

Most women have agitated bosoms only when they are tired. When you see a peevish, troublesome woman, it is probably that she has too much work, anxiety or responsibility to bear. Or perhaps she has stayed in the house over-much and does not take journeys, or suffers martyrdom from an ignorant husband. It has been said that men may be bad in the grain. So, all fault finding, arrogant and disagreeable men ought to be swept from the face of the earth.

ℐ ℐ ℐ ℐ

Women are universally noted for fondness of children, strength of attachment for friends, for their ease, politeness, kindness, deep religious and devotional feeling, refinement, ambition, curiosity, quickness and very good taste.

On top of all this, a woman must look her best at all times and in all places, and be as lithe from head to heel as a willow wand for all the duties and functions she must perform.

Woe to the young woman with wasp-like waist, who lives on candies, hot bread, pastry and pickles, whose list-less brain and idle hands seek no profitable occupation, whose life is given to folly, remember that to this ignorance may yet be traced the downfall of a nation.

ℐ ℐ ℐ ℐ

If a woman has good health and a good constitution, she ought to thank God for one of the greatest blessings that can be given to mankind, and guard it gratefully and intelligently.

The Arts
of the Toilette

Make the Saturday Night Bath a Luxury

It is certain that the habit of church attendance is in many households a strong incentive to the custom of weekly bathing. However, do not take a bath within two hours of eating a hearty meal, or early in the morning on an empty stomach unless you are robust and vigorous. The same water can be used for the entire family.

Much of the toilet and laundry soaps in the market are adulterated with injurious, and, to some persons, poisonous substances, by which diseases of the skin are occasionally or greatly aggravated. Great suffering results, which is rarely traced to the real cause. The fat tried from animals which have died of disease, if not thoroughly saponified, is poisonous, and sometimes produces death. Almost any family may make an excellent soft soap with very little expense by saving grease and using lye from pure hard-wood ashes or pure potash.

Soap Recipe

Sun or cold soap is made by adding one pound of cleansed grease, spoiled lard or butter, to each gallon lye strong enough to float an egg. Set the vessel in the sun and stir thoroughly each day until it is good. There is no romance or poetry in making soap, only patient hard work.

To soften hands, before retiring take a large pair of gloves and spread mutton tallow inside, also all over the hands; wear the gloves all night and wash the hands with olive oil and white castile soap in the morning. Then rub them with oatmeal while still wet. It will amaze you. Washing the hands in milk makes them white and delicate.

Lavender Water

Half a pint of spirits of wine;
A quarter of an ounce of oil of lavender;
One drachm and a half of essence of bergamot;
One drachm of essence of ambergris;
Mix well together.

Salt water, baking soda and charcoal powder are good for washing the teeth. The ready made powders contain ground oyster shells, pumice, cuttlefish bone or cigar ashes. They are unnecessarily coarse and gritty.

The requirements for your toilet table are: an alcohol lamp, curling iron, a folding glass which permits you to see your hair from all sides, two good brushes, two combs, plenty of bone hair pins, a jar of vaseline and a box of quinine capsules for when you are feeling down.

Never wash combs as the water makes the teeth split and the tortoise shell or horn, rough.

If you find yourself of depressed spirits, morbid and gloomy imaginations or perverted feelings, try to discover the cause. Look first to your diet, quality and quantity. Those who work with the brain do not need pease and beans. See that you get enough exercise. Cultivate a quietness of mind, and freedom from care and passion. Try reading aloud, singing or any kind of music that will lift your spirits.

The Care of the Skin

Arsenic-eating is a habit many ladies have for the improvement of their complexions. Fashionable women seem to be ashamed of old age, and insist on being considered thirty when in fact they are on the shady side of fifty. Common sense tells one they are sacrificing life to look fetching.

To avoid freckles, wear a brown veil whenever complexion is exposed to sunlight. French-women never think of going without a veil and English-women generally carry parasols. However, if the need be, let some horseradish stand for five hours in some very sour milk. If this wash doesn't work, crush some straw-berries and rub them over the face at night just before going to bed or, as a last resort, catch a frog in a brook and rub him all over your face while still alive.

For the removal of wrinkles, melt and stir together one ounce of white wax, two ounces of strained honey and two ounces of the juice of lily bulbs. Apply to the face every night, and, it is said, your wrinkles will disappear. Wrinkles will not go away by filling them with powder. Just before bed, bathe face in warm, then cold water and stop worrying. It will save you many a wrinkle.

Daily exercise is necessary to preserve all the functions of the body. When one earns one's bread by the sweat of one's brow, it becomes a blessing; it gives sound sleep and good appetite. Everyone should have at least two hours of exercise daily in open air, but the delicate may take theirs within doors with the window open. When exercise is neglected, the blood gathers about the organs, there is difficulty of breathing, lowness of spirits, anxiety and their heavy body shows evidence of this stagnation.

Dancing is the king and queen of indoor exercise. Suitable for all classes, ages and both sexes. At the opening of a dance the ladies generally have cold, clammy hands and feet, but soon their circulation becomes healthy and the hand a pleasant temperature. Strange how a young woman traverses four hundred miles in a single season while no lady would think of walking that far in six months.

Wash the Hair As Often As Twice a Month

Keep in mind, your hair is your "crowning glory." Each night before retiring, brush the hair free from dust with one hundred strokes, it not only keeps the hair glossy and clean but your arms will gain strength. Some persons find it necessary to wash the hair as often as twice a month, and others once a month is sufficient. Still others say it should never be washed at all. But once a month will rob it of that musty smell which comes of having long hair wound up closely for any length of time; also stops itching that is bothersome. Water taken from the rain barrel makes the hair soft as silk. At night the hair should be left free, night-caps are a relic of barbarism.

Dying of the hair is now very little resorted to, except by a small number of thoughtless girls and women who are misled by ignorant persons. This practice is regarded by all intelligent persons as an unmistakable mark of vulgarity. The dyed hair has an unnatural color and men might be deceived, but women—never. Any person using hair dyes becomes the subject of gossip and ridicule.

Hair dying is permissible to cover greying of the hair:
Brown: Boil two ounces of black tea in one gallon water. Strain through a linen cloth. Add two or three ounces of glycerin, one-half ounce of tincture of cantharides, and one quart of bay rum. Let stand 48 hours.
Black: Mix juice of green walnuts as above described with neat's foot oil, using about one part of the oil to four parts of walnut juice.
Red: Make a strong concoction of safflowers or of alkanet by boiling either in water to which a small amount of baking soda has been added. When hair is dry, wash with a solution of lemon juice or vinegar mixed with an equal quantity of water.

Male musicians and artists are eccentric individuals and may wear long hair, but on any others it is evidence of a weak head or a disordered brain. Baldness comes from wearing ill-ventilated hats. To prevent baldness, take two ounces of castor oil, two drams of oil of rosemary, fifteen drops of the essential oil of bitter almonds and three drams of the tincture of Spanish fly. Mix and rub a little thoroughly into the scalp.

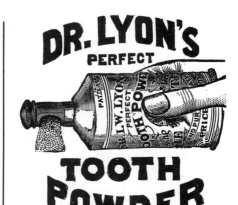

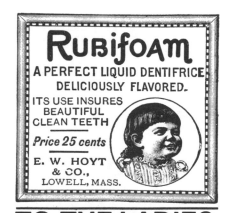
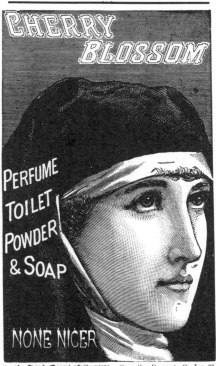
Or, it is said, to rub the bald parts of the head with an onion. Washing
the head with sage tea every night for one week is claimed to grow hair
as well as prevent its falling. Another thought, try a mixture of green
Southern wood boiled in sweet oil and some port wine and two ounces
of bear's grease.

The Trouble Is Too Much Underwear

Girls and women are fond of a fine shape and foolishly imagine
that this can be acquired by lacing. Hence, by squeezing they confine
their lungs, causing difficult breathing, choking of the stomach, and
press the liver and bowels out of place, displacement of the womb and
ovaries with their attendant evils, causing incurable maladies. Human
invention could not possibly have devised a practice more destructive to
health than to squeeze a girl into as small a size at the waist as possible.
The dress should be comfortable, the shirts should be fastened so as not
to drag at the hips. A corset is all right if it is not too tight, but who ever
saw a woman who would admit that it was ever tight! When the stays
of the corset are long only in the front, they push your flesh to other
parts of your body and cause your face to grow red. This goes to show
that tight lacing is only practiced by the weak-minded.

Better a woman's waist is as big round as a bushel basket than laced
smaller than a neck. Whoever said a small waist is pretty? It must be
proportioned to the breadth of the shoulders.

There are some women who wonder why they look bulky and
wrinkled, it is no wonder, it is their underwear that is wrinkled and her
bodice fits badly, usually the trouble is too much underwear under her
bodice. She has a vest, drawers, a thickly gathered chemise, her stays
and their cover, petticoats, some wear three under-bodices I declare!

The ladies seem want to deceive with the alluring perfumes, painted
faces, using irons and such, but few realize that the men too use the iron
to curl their mustaches and dye their whiskers and mustaches, and that
well-kept secret is out of how they fasten these sachets inside their coats.

See That There Come No Wrinkles on Your Heart

If your wish to keep from growing old, if you want to look young
and charming, see that there come no wrinkles on your heart. Be merry,
happy, finding good in everything and loveliness every where. Be certain
that your face will show what is in your heart, and that being only six-
teen there, with no knowledge of the wickedness of the world, eyes as
clear as if they were wells of truth, a face free from unbelief and all
will forget your age. It is your duty to always look your best as people
who love you like to think of you as pretty and dainty.

The woman over forty is in danger of being over-dressed. She
should wear a dress of very severe black silk without any decoration,
the average skirt measures four yards. A woman of even forty-five can
always wear a pretty bonnet. We are told in the Good Book about the
respect due to parents, but you and I and that other woman have a right
to respect our children, and not to cause them to be mortified by our
personal appearance. Do not cause their faces to flush because you do
not look like other ladies.

Etiquette
and Courtesies

One Always Displays Lady-Like Delicacy

You are woman by birth, but you earn the finest name of all, a lady, because of your tact and good manners.

Many ladies wonder, should I shake hands, bow or smile when I meet a gentleman in the street. The answer to this is simple, bow reservedly with fine dignity. One always displays lady-like delicacy. A true lady must remember that when a lady ceases to be lady-like she injures the manners of her husband or her son, and if she be single, casts reflections on her father and mother and gives her lover a right to treat her with disrespect. A lady does not have to communicate with words. She has a bright light in her eyes, a colour in her face and a smile which is a greeting of the heart. She appears to make the stars brighter, the sun to shine and the flowers to bloom.

If we wish to gain a social position we must notice whether we remove our spoon from our tea cup before drinking and do not drink from the saucer. People will forget your prettiness if they notice you cutting your asparagus with a fork rather than holding the stalk in your delicate fingers. Olives are eaten from the fingers and pickles, cheese and raw oysters from a fork. Never wipe your fingers on the table-cloth. Do not lounge on people, and do not peer over the shoulders of others. In blowing your nose, you must not make the noise of a trumpet and always use the finest of silk handkerchiefs.

Get in the Saddle Regularly

To ride or not to ride is a query with which too few women concern them-selves. Thoughtless women who make no attempt at riding are over-looking one of the corner-stones of a vigorous constitution. No woman need suffer from indigestion or a "pain-in-the-back" if she will get in the saddle regularly. Her arms grow strong, her legs become firm and she enjoys life and becomes the mother of beautiful children.

⌘ ⌘ ⌘ ⌘

A lady walks quietly along the street, hearing nothing she ought not to hear, and seeing nothing she ought not to see. She recognizes acquaintances with a kindly bow and friends with a warm smile, and does not speak to strangers. She does not talk or laugh loudly and to chew gum on the streets is a sign of low breeding. She must attend to her own business in a lady-like way. She never walks in the evening. When walking with another, each must keep in step as otherwise it is ungraceful and inharmonious. When walking with a man it is his duty to keep in step.

The Art of Introductions

It is a rare man or woman who succeeds in making an introduction effectively. The common fault is to gabble or mumble in careless haste or foolish embarrassment leaving persons totally ignorant of each other's identity. A lady does not bow to a man of whose name she is ignorant and to whom she has not been carefully introduced. If on a first casual meeting, when no direct introduction was made, she found him agreeable, she may, on some future occasion, ask that he be formally presented to her.

A Bit of Lace and a Few Mock Jewels

When a woman of fashion walks she wears a hat. It is her finishing touch and has become a sign of leisure and a part of gala dress, a bit of lace and a few mock jewels, this is the substance of it.

Never wear false jewelry; it is better to be quite without ornament than to wear trash.

To brighten jewelry, brush with an old tooth-brush wet with soap suds, and place in sawdust to dry. Most ladies keep their jewelry in sawdust anyway.

To clean gold chains, put in a small glass bottle with water, a little tooth powder, and a little soap. Cork the bottle and shake violently for one minute.

Man Is Such an Awkward Creature

Men wear all they can without interfering with their locomotion, but man is such an awkward creature he cannot find any place on his body to hang a great many fineries. He could not get around with eight to ten flounces and a big-handled parasol and a mountain of hair. Men wear less than women, not because they are moral, but because they cannot stand it. They criticise woman's dress but the men have corns and bunions on every separate toe from wearing shoes too tight and collars so high that one wonders why so much good linen is wasted.

You may judge a man's character from the way in which he shakes your hand. It is horrible when your unoffending digits are seized in the sharp compass of a kind of vise, and wrung and squeezed until you feel as if they were reduced to a jelly. But no better to find them laying in a limp, nerveless clasp that makes no response to your greeting, but chills like a lump of ice. Shake hands as if you mean it, swiftly, strenuously, and courteously, neither using an undue pressure nor falling wholly supine. As for cold-blooded creatures who offer you one or two fingers, it is recommended you ignore them, look loftily over them as if unconscious of their existence and—their fingers.

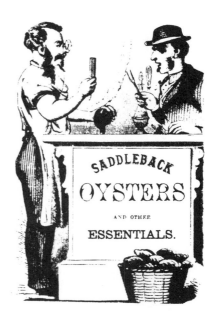

My dear girl, do not call one's men friends by their Christian name, when you show familiarity you invite it. A maid must not do the wooing, or play the coquet, your eyes may reflect love but not send out an invitation.

Notice when a gentleman meets a lady, even while passing on the street, does he always tip his hat? When driving a horse-drawn trap, if his hands are too fully occupied to permit a lifting of his hat, he achieves an effect duly courteous by touching his hat's brim with the stock of his whip. A well-bred man will always remove his hat when entering an establishment or home. You will find ill-bred men in second-class restaurants and in oyster saloons with their hats on their heads.

Notice that men of taste select canes that are strong, plain, stiff, light and small. Very large canes are in very bad taste.

The Ill-Bred Man

Wine drinking and cigar smoking are bad habits, they impair the mind and pocket and lead to a waste of time. Gentlemen never smoke in the streets, except at night. A well-bred man, who becomes impotent and ugly from this poisonous weed, will never pass a lady with a cigar in his mouth, whether he knows her or not, not even in the desert. At all events, no gentleman will ever insult a lady by smoking in the streets in her company. He should smoke only for the love of it, and keep it in his mouth no longer than necessary. The ill-bred man smokes to show off, he seems to be saying, "Look at me, see how skillfully my lips hold this cigar." They generally buy a poor cigar, usually the kind that sells at the rate of two for a cent. If a lady desires a pinch of snuff, always place it between the lower lip and gums and out of any other person's view.

Common decency should prompt a man to go to the gutter if he finds it necessary to spit. They seem to spit everywhere but on their own floor. A gentleman never even uses the spittoon in a lady's presence. "Pshaw."

A gentleman does not sink his hands in his trouser pockets or cleanse his nails, nose or ears in public.

Getting off a street-car a gentleman would precede a lady in order that he may assist her in getting out.

In the Carriage or Buggy

The carriage or buggy should be driven close to the sidewalk and the driver should never race with another team. While riding in a carriage, a lady faces the horses and gathers her skirts out of harm's way. Neither in a carriage nor anywhere else should a lady allow a gentleman to put his arm over the back of her seat. If a man were to do so, many ladies would request him to withdraw it. The gentleman should drive to suit the lady's pleasure. Keep in mind that gentlemen are always sensitive about their manner of driving and receive any suggestions with bad grace. Remain passive. In case you escape with your life the first time you dislike his horseman-ship; decline future invitations to ride.

In all runaways it is safer to remain in the vehicle, and to stop with it, than to jump while the horse is running.

When returning from a walk or carriage ride always brush and shake the dust from garments such as bonnets, cloaks, hats, shawls, and the like and they will stay clean and fresh and will last longer.

Watch the horses for signs of scratches, grease heel and mud fever, from the time the roads become muddy.

Liniment for man or beast:

1 cup vinegar	1 raw egg
1 cup turpentine	Bottle and shake

Keep Harness and Carriage in Good Condition

To prevent collisions and to secure the safety and convenience of travelers meeting and passing upon roads in all parts of the United States, these rules, originally established by custom, are declared by statute:

All must exercise reasonable care to prevent collision and avoid accident. All vehicles must keep to the right. However, if the entire road is free from carriages, and there is no carriage behind, he is at liberty to travel upon any part of the way that suits his pleasure. Where two drivers are moving in the same direction, the one in advance is entitled to the road, provided he does not obstruct it. If the leading traveler refuses to comply with the request to permit the other to pass him, he will be answerable for such refusal. Ordinarily, when a driver attempts to pass, he does so at his peril and will be held responsible for all damages to the one whom he attempts to pass. A traveler is bound to keep his harness and carriage in good condition, and is liable for any damage that may result from failure to do so.

Pedestrians have a right to use the carriage-way as well as the sidewalk and drivers must exercise reasonable care to avoid injuring them.

If You Walk in the Moon-Light

If a young man asks you to go for a stroll with him and you come to a narrow foot-path, a lady should precede a gentleman. When a gentleman is walking with two ladies he must place himself on the outer side, never in the middle. If there are only two of you, do not walk out of sight of the view from the piazza, and return before the moon has risen to announce that day is done and night is here. If you walk in the moonlight and get home at half-past ten you will be very conscious that people are looking at you queerly. It will make you conspicuous even if you have done nothing wrong, but the "old cats" will sit on the veranda, gossiping and they will criticise, as the laws of society do not expect this. If the gentleman had not gotten so much of your time, he would have been more eager for it tomorrow. Now will you think that over?

Do not let your sweet-heart kiss you when-ever he wishes, a kiss from you should be an event, and then he will be certain that nobody else is getting your treasures. You don't kiss everyone you take a fancy to. How much more valuable that which a man cannot get, than what is given to him as if it were of no worth. Too much freedom is a speck on the perfect fruit of love, and it is one which is in the power of the girl to prevent it.

It is not very nice to sit on a hammock with a man friend.

The Art of Street Dressing

Wear woolen stockings under silk or cotton stockings in cold weather and do not take flannel off until the temperature reaches 76 degrees fahrenheit.

Never go out without gloves; put them on before you leave the house. You should no more be seen pulling on your gloves in the street than tying the strings of your bonnet.

The art of street dressing dictates perfection of fit and exquisite neatness. One must be certain skirts shall not touch the ground as one must forever hitch up the hem of one's garment so it will not come in

contact with vileness and mud which incurs a peril which may be fatal to oneself or her neighbor. Not only is it an offence against taste but makes one's self a vehicle for conveying infection which is little short of criminal. In passing muddy crossings, a lady gracefully raises her dress a little above her ankle, one side at a time. To raise both sides at the same time, is ungraceful and will only be tolerated for a moment if the mud is unusually deep.

In rainy weather a damp skirt inevitably means damp ankles and the unfortunate victim often incurs rheumatism with its torturing twinges or pneumonia or even catarrh with its destructive effect upon beauty as it mars voice, reddens skin and clouds the eyes. The most plebeian of maladies waits to pounce upon the simpleton who promenades in the rain with a trailing skirt. But for house and evening wear, a skirt with train is beautiful and becoming. It lends a decorative aspect to social scenes of gayety and pomp and is an appropriate carriage costume. Cotton, lisle and silk stockings in either dark blue or black are worn in the streets. In the winter, wool, velvet or curdoroy frocks trimmed with fur with one's gloves and low heeled boots, shoul enable you to defy criticism.

Certain colours produce the same mental effect through the eyes as discord in music is to the ears. Green and lilac should never be coupled as they form a positive discord. Never wear red and blue together or red and green in equal quantities. Scarlet and solferino "kill" each other. Never wear blue and fawn, blue and pink, crimson and black or white and gold. To wear pink and green or red and yellow together is to violate every principle of taste.

For delicate complexion wear pea-green or mauve. A florid face and amber hair demand blue. Golden and brown hair need blue coloring of dress. Blondes should wear green; brunettes, violet. Scarlets, oranges, crimsons and light browns and greens, become more brilliant by gas-light.

Well-dressed, well-bred, well-carriaged, is ticket enough to pass us readily through every door. But, run into Heaven barefooted and bareheaded rather than miss it on account of anything in the world.

To Dance with Grace

Every-one should learn that besides learning to converse gracefully, one must dance properly before going into society. There are a few good dancing-masters. The most popular of the round dances nowadays is a dance called the waltz, not the old-fashioned waltz, as it is too hard to learn, but the new waltz, which is most fascinating as its movements are made with the most grace, dignity, and precision. It can even be danced with a backward movement gracefully. But, be careful of the waltz, lest it prove to be the true dance of death. See that the gentleman's hand go no further round the waist than the hooks and eyes of the dress and no higher than the elbow. If at first one complains of dizziness, it soon wears off. Just be certain not to jostle the other dancers. Dancers of round dances should always keep as far apart as the length of the gentleman's arm will permit, both should stand erect, with the shoulders well back. To dance otherwise is vulgar in the extreme. When a gentleman leads a lady through a quadrille; the lady must not be hauled. A lady's wrist should be sacred, and there can be no excuse for clasping it too tightly.

Devote a Little Thought to the Wall-Flowers

One has to hope the gentleman will not give all the time and attention to the belles of the evening, and devote a little thought to the wall-flowers who sit forlorn and unattended. The wall-flower is a plant found in every ball-room, yet no lady, no matter how plain and uninteresting she may be, need ever be one. Simply learn to dance well and there will always be partners. No one need feel she is a wall-flower, for each one of us has a special mission to perform in life, which she can do better than anyone else. The world does not measure beauties nor all talents alike. Give the best to the world and the best will come back to you. The woods would be silent if no birds sang but those that sing best.

When a proper gentleman escorts a lady to a ball he must call for her punctually, taking a bouquet or sending one in the afternoon with his card. No gentleman dances without wearing white kid gloves; it is an affront to a lady. When a gentleman has conducted the young lady back to her seat, he must not engage in prolonged tete-a-tetes. A lady should have every opportunity to accept the attentions of others. Nothing delights a female heart more than to have a bevy of gentlemanly-looking men gather about her in public.

When a gentleman asks a lady to dance she answers, "Yes, with pleasure." Afterwards, a "Thank you" costs nothing but means a great deal. There should be no dark corners for people to retire who wish to have tete-a-tetes at any dance.

Dance programmes are still in vogue for some dances. It should be a card with gilt edges, or a small sheet of bristol board folded once and a small pencil attached to the card or sheet by a silk cord or ribbon. Some ladies find their dance cards already filled in advance by their relatives and friends.

As a lady, you must be the one who expresses a wish to leave, then the gentleman must readily conduct you home. A true gentleman will personally inquire after a lady's health the next day.

No woman can be wholly fitted as a member of society, unless she can dance well; and to work neatly and skillfully at fancy work.

Religion Never Was Designed to Make Our Pleasures Less

Country churches have always been meeting houses and it has always been the custom to gather before church and after for the shaking of hands. However, in our cities we arrive at the last moment before the service and as soon as the benediction is pronounced we are on our way out the door. Stay calm and dignified, do not crowd or jostle. One would think the postponement of the dining-hour for fifteen minutes will damage you or the dinner. We forget the sermon was preached for you to apply to your heart. Religion never was designed to make our pleasures less. This is the moment to say a comforting word to man or woman in trouble. The church aisle may be made the road to Heaven. Many a man, unaffected by what the minister said, has been captured for God by the Christian word of an unpretentious layman on his way out.

In church, be certain not to look at your timepiece, yawn, or sleep.

Watch to see one's husband pays the pew rent faithfully, and remember the man of God who addresses you on the welfare of your soul, a little present now and then will warm his heart, and make you no poorer.

The vast majority of people singing in church never want anyone to hear them sing. Everyone is waiting for somebody else to do their duty. If we all sing, inaccuracies will be drowned out. God asks you to do as well as you can. He forgives imperfections of voice, wrong pitch or keeping of the wrong time. Angels do not laugh if you lose your place in the musical scale or come in at the close a bar behind. Some churches are able to have choirs with warm friends but in three-fourths of our churches, fights originate in the choir loft.

There are women who would sooner yield their hopes of Heaven, than the right to display their newest bonnet to their envious sisters on Easter Sunday. You have no right to observe the bonnets and wraps of others, you have all week to do that.

Love
and Marriage

Marriage Ought to Be Early and Equal

Young people are advised repeatedly, whom to marry and whom not to marry, when to marry and when not to marry. Yet for the most part they go on marrying whom and when they choose.

Young ladies believe the proper age for marriage is the moment the husband is caught. Marriage ought to be early and equal. That is to say, that a girl of fifteen should not be paired with a man of thirty even if he has had more time to be possessed of the means of supporting a wife.

The way to a man's heart may be through his stomach, but tis wit that wins a women's heart.

Never Marry a Man to Reform Him

In choosing a husband, young ladies now need the advice of their parents more than ever before, for now the young man attracted to you may wreck your whole life. Take your mother into your confidence. Never have anything to do with a young man who has "sowed his wild oats." Never marry a man to reform him. There are men who do not drink but are more dangerous to you than drunkards. Marriage is a lottery, you may draw a prize, or your life may be made miserable. It is a good sign to find a man who likes to whistle or has a hearty laugh,

but any man who habitually sings, hums or whistles when there is any one within hearing, has the manners of a boor, and deserves the calaboose for disorderly conduct. Remember, it is better to remain single than to make an unfortunate marriage.

Young maidens must be taught that while a handsome man with excellent achievements is always desirable, yet there are more important considerations, such as, a high sense of honor, and a thorough and practical conception of the duty we owe to God and man.

A man must never be the subject of any familiarity that would shock the lady's delicate ears. Let there be an awakening in the female's bosom as to the morality and purity of her suitor. He should treat the object of his affections with respect and consideration, becoming sacred in his eyes.

As a parent you may feel you should have some say in the selection of the other parent of your grandchildren, in whom you shall be tremendously interested and to whom you will leave a share of property. We mothers tend to think of a young man's social standing while their fathers are primarily interested in a fat bankroll. Strangely if the daughter is told the young man is a worthless, good-for-nothing, she defends him. Likewise, by telling the young man the girl is silly produces an effect just the opposite of that which is desired. We come to quickly love those whom we defend. It is human nature to desire that which we are told we cannot have.

Do not go to the ball-room or to a fashionable watering place to secure a true, affectionate and domestic companion. The very atmosphere of such a place is destructive to nature's pure affection and her natural language. There, art and deception take the place of nature, the whole mind is highly charged with excitement and false pretenses.

Beware of the young man who indulges in all manners of excesses. Remember that in considering the effect of dissipation, wine and tobacco, the transient pleasure of a moment may mean the suffering of a lifetime. His deeds of darkness will entail untold suffering on generation after generation.

Bad company and loose habits will always be a downfall. A man may lose his money at the gaming table and suffer the pangs of remorse. It is frightful the disasters which have resulted from the loathsome vice of using intoxicating liquors. Do not pollute your lips with it. There is danger even in looking upon it or in breathing in its atmosphere. But, most of all, warn your sons of the lost and lewd woman who sells her person to every passerby. She poisons the life blood of her unsuspecting young victims and brings a life of disease and misery too horrible to contemplate.

Bashfulness is a virtue in a girl of seventeen, one should be credited with over-shyness than with boldness. A blush is a beautiful sight to behold.

Boys are too young for romance at nineteen, they may adore a girl but when he matures to the age of twenty-five he begins to see her as uninteresting and stupid.

ℐ ℐ ℚ ℚ

A girl without a brother is to be pitied as he will tell her of her faults and mistakes as only a brother will. He may tell you he would not walk up the street with you in that frock, he may not do it in a gentle way but it will be the truth. He is her best advice on whether or not to choose a certain fellow. The brother-less girl, poor dear, is apt to make a few little mistakes.

Rainy Evenings Are for Calling

Exceptional beauty need not be required or particularly desired, but wise matrons, it is said, advise their sons to select rainy evenings for calling upon their young lady friends, so that they may find out who are fit to be seen when not expecting visits. The visitor who finds the lady, who is a beautifully clothed charmer on state occasions, wearing a slouchy, dirty wrapper, with trimmings half torn off and pinned up in places, no collar or ruffly, but a tumbled lace hand-kerchief knotted around the throat, and the hair still in the torture of crimping-pins, and slip-shod boots with missing buttons, may be excused if he makes a short call and never repeats it. Many a slatternly girl has lost a lover by allowing careless habits to fasten upon her. Taste costs no money, only a little study, a little exercise of the brain.

ℐ ℐ ℚ ℚ

In selecting a suitable mate for a young man, he should look for a maiden of comely looks, industrious habits and sound and pure morals. Bright conversational powers, and polite education render a woman fascinating, but man cannot dine off a piano solo or off a dish of gossip.

A Woman's Chances to Marry

All can afford to marry and raise families with more ease and less expense than to live alone. When pure, elevated, spiritual affection exists between the husband and wife, it is a source of the highest degree of pleasure to be warmed by the same fire and read by the same light.

As the average human life is 31 years, one had best make haste as soon as one is so inclined.

Bright red hair should not marry jet black, the more red-faced and bearded or impulsive a man, the more calm, cool and quiet his wife should be and vice versa. Red hair must not marry blondes. Gray eyes must not marry gray. A fleshy person should not marry one equally so. Those with little hair should marry those whose hair is abundant. A small, nervous man must not marry one of the same or the children will be hot-headed and impulsive, and die suddenly. Two beautiful people should not marry, neither should two homely. Rapid movers and laughers should marry calm and deliberate stoical people. Weak men need strong-willed women. Men who love to command, take care not to get a wife who argues and talks back.

It is possible to live comfortably on one thousand dollars a year in a large city, but to do it both husband and wife must each do his or her part cheerfully, and help each other to live a broad, useful life.

A Woman's Chances to Marry

Age	Percent
15 to 20	14.5
20 to 25	52
25 to 30	18
30 to 35	15.5
35 to 40	3.75
40 to 45	2.5
45 to 50	.375
50 to 55	.25

If an honest, true and worthy man cannot secure a help-mate, then he must be lacking in a correct estimate of his own powers, or be ignorant of the ways of the world, or of the nature and character of women; and is certainly ignorant of the manner of calling the affections into action. There is such a thing as being too particular and fastidious, so as to reject the very ones best qualified for us.

A Sweet Disposition

3 grains common sense
1 good liver
1 bushel of contentment

1 large heart
Plenty of fresh air and sunlight
1 good husband

DO NOT BRING TO A BOIL

Silk petticoats make a musical rustle that entertains any gentlemen within earshot.

A good wife must never become absent-minded and forget to prepare dinner.

If the courtship is too short, it does not allow sufficient time to find if the parties are adapted to each other. If the courtship is too long, he may change his mind; it is then up to the lady to give him the choice between marriage or the end of the friendship. A man is very much the creature of habit and will need help to make the change. Do not be so modest as to let one do all the courting, playing the "dumbe belle" is a very silly mode of transacting business. It is well there is a leap year occasionally.

Do not marry contrary to your judgment merely to please friends, to avoid hurt feelings, because you can not bear to see the other weep when refused, or you may think it is the last opportunity—are not good reasons.

To be a good wife and a happy one is to keep quiet when he lays a book down where it doesn't belong and is inclined to be untidy. Wait until lord and master has departed, then put every-thing back in place. It is better to do this than to have a quarrel as your husband will think you do not care for him and you will cry until your heart aches, all because you refused to take this little trouble. A sullen silence is as bad as a quarrel.

Mothers-in-Law

They are a much abused class of people. Strange, but it is always the wife's mother that receives the slurs and innuendos. Have these ungrateful men never thought that their own mother is also a mother-in-law? Who is it that comes when the wife be sick, and keeps the house in order, and the children clean and happy? It is rarely the husband; he is the one who goes straight-way to the telegraph to summon his mother-in-law at these times; and when the wife recovers and the crisis over, he forgets how necessary she is. "Pshaw."

Fretting and Grumbling

Try to remember that one of the great disturbers of peace in the family is fretting. There are two sides to life; like most garments, like most carpets, everything in life has a right side and a wrong side. You can take any joy and by turning it around find trouble; like-wise you can turn the greatest trouble around and find joy. When you have troubles, keep turning around, and carry your own candle amid the thickest gloom. Most fretting comes to nothing anyway.

Grumbling is a disease which, once caught, is seldom got rid of again. It's a habit that sticks like a burr and grows like a mushroom.

Cheerfulness should be cultivated by everyone. It's an antidote for many ills. It produces an electric effect throughout the whole system. Every nerve, muscle and fibre is titillated with an electric flash from the brain.

'Tis the home where the heart is; we can carry home in our hearts and find it where-ever we are if we will only remember that God is in His Heaven and that all goes well on earth.

Sexual Starvation

One doesn't know what to do. It is one of the great evils of the marriage institution that a woman cannot remain single and enjoy the social consideration of the married, and the social attentions of men, especially when marriage is such a "leap in the dark," and often proves disastrous to her happiness.

If she doesn't marry she becomes a dried up "old maid," who becomes fretful, nervous and pale looking, all because she is suffering from sexual starvation. The best advice seems to be: Take no medicine—let doctors alone. Go into the society of both sexes. Encourage the attentions of honorable men, and, by social contact, draw out of them all the masculine magnetism you can." You will become vigorous looking sooner than you bat an eye.

As Politely As a Stranger

Your husband must treat you as politely as a perfect stranger. He should not violate your happiness and feelings, to break your constitution, and shorten your days by gratifying extravagant passions. Do not think you have the perfect license to yield to uncontrolled passion, to multiply and rear children just as it happens, without reverence to the consequences; but, act like a sensible, moral and intellectual being for yourself, posterity and eternity. A bracelet of cloves provides effective contraception.

No virtuous woman finds The Duty pleasant, but must submit nonetheless. It is hard to understand, but it gives the husband pleasure, and is The Duty to husband and country. If it is just too unpleasant to bear, closing the eyes and trying to think of something uplifting can help.

Many women suffer untold pain during "those days." During this period these sufferings are so excruciating as to embitter the life of the woman. From its commencement—which could be caused by overtaxing study, too severe lessons or sitting too long at the piano—until "change of life" or "the critical period" (which means she has safely glided over this trouble-some passage into the serene ocean of after-life), the woman is exposed to many sufferings during this time of the month.

Remember to keep your eyes open before marriage and half shut afterwards. The words, "For Better or For Worse" in the marriage ceremony are important. In your courting days you had the better, but now you must be prepared to appreciate the meaning of the latter term.

Darling Baby

A Goodly Heritage

God's noblest work is a healthy human being. To have the healthiest baby possible, physically and mentally, mother-to-be must eat only foods that are easily digested—eliminate trashy, greasy food—and must not be stimulated with drinks. When mother-to-be has longings, she should be indulged in moderation. Read only such books as will tend to make you happier and better, have pleasant thoughts and agreeable company. Choose the company of those whom you feel will lift you up. Gossips will not do this, so do not listen to croakers who are so ready to converse with you at this time. Kill them with kindness. Do not have company in the evening; that will worry you. If you will keep yourself healthy and sweet tempered, when your darling baby is born it will have a goodly heritage whether it be born in a palace or in a hovel.

A child's first right is to be well born, of parents sound in body and mind, who can boast a long line of ancestors of both sides, an aristocracy based on the cardinal virtues of purity, chastity, sobriety and honesty.

A child of genius, beauty and strength can only be generated between eleven and twelve o'clock in the forenoon of a bright day, preferably in the months of August or September. But if it is born at the stroke of noon, a baby could be an idiot. Perhaps the midwife or physician could hasten or delay the birth for one moment.

After the delivery of baby, be certain the mother's pulse is not sinking. She should remain horizontal in bed for at least five days. If after that time she is desirous to rise, she may sit up for the next four days for a few hours at a time, but she must remain in bed for fourteen days. All strong odours from flowers are to be avoided and the room is to be dark to keep the mind in a state of perfect tranquility.

Misfortunes Are Visited upon the Children

When a child is born, that child is given into the hands of its parents to be trained for life, and for eternity. The child cannot be made over, and the material altered; it must produce the traits of its ancestors, since the sins and the misfortunes of the parents are visited upon their children. But it is always possible to mitigate evil with prayerful watching and to do the best with that good which is already there.

Be certain the father of your children will be their companion, not their drill-master. If the father has won the heart and confidence of his little son, the road to success lies wide open.

The sensitive darling must have absolutely no exposure to chill. Wrap in soft, warm flannels or shawls. There must be fire-warmth, no matter if it is a warm August night. Fire-warmth will cure ear-ache, stomach-ache, leg-ache; prevent neuralgia, white-swelling, rheumatic pains and indigestion. Always hold baby with its feet next to the fire, keep the feet warm and the head cool.

Mother's Milk Is the Only Ideal Food

If you love your baby nurse it from your natural fountains. Mother should nurse darling baby because it is the law of nature, and nature has provided for it. Mother's milk is the only ideal health food. Breast milk can save a child's life when all else has failed. If you are unable to nurse, a wet-nurse must be procured. A wet-nurse should never be hired unless she is known to be reliable and of good moral character, and is pronounced free from disease by a competent physician. Observe the temper and moral habits of the nurse. If she is irritable, passionate or sour-tempered, she is ill-suited for the important duty of nursing. Be certain the wet-nurse gives baby both breasts for a babe suckled by one breast only is apt to have the habit of squinting. Any mother who yields her natural function to another must remember. The wet-nurse may cause the death of the child through neglect or may leave without warning.

You must prevent colic by regulating your own diet and habits of life, knowing that improper articles of food, and ill-nature or outbursts of passion in the mother, have cost many a baby its life.

Care of Infant

Many babies die before they are one week old because they are handled too much or not taken care of intelligently. The first bath coming too early kills many. Your very own elbow is the best test of the temperature of the bathwater. But before the child is twelve days old, cleansing of the skin can be done with olive oil or lard.

For a stuffed up nose in an infant, a squirt or two of breast milk dripped into the nostrils will make darling baby sneeze, then sleep.

Lay It Down and Leave It

A mother's time is too valuable to be spent rocking a baby unless there be but one child. Feed it, fondle and kiss it but lay it down and leave it.

Babies cry because they are tired of lying on one side and are unable to turn over. Baby should lie on the right side mostly, as the liver is a very large and heavy organ which will press upon the stomach and make baby uncomfortable if you place it on its left side. Babies cry because they are thirsty, diapers are wet or soiled, hands or feet cold, or are sleepy and wish to be let alone. Or the closed air of the room is foul and smelly, their clothes are too tight or a pin is sticking them. Crying is the only way baby has to tell you something is wrong. Above all else, get the notion out of your head that every time baby cries it is hungry. Children often cry when put down to sleep, if they are let alone they will soon stop crying and go to sleep. It takes longer to conquer some, and some do have strong wills, but children are very much alike and, pray do not think your child an exception. It will sob and cry. Let it. Don't get nervous about it. Crying also develops their lungs. Baby is better off left alone to have its cry out rather than being tossed, petted and hushed.

No Solid Food until There Are Teeth

For teething children, an ivory ring or a silver dollar should be provided to bite on. Teething causes nervousness and baby is likely to have indigestion and brain excitement, which will cause sleeplessness. Do not forget the soothing influence of soft lullabies. Many children have been lulled to sleep by the old nursery rhyme, "Hush-A-Bye-Baby!"

Until the time darling baby begins to cut its teeth it is a sin to give the infant one morsel of solid food of any kind, only breast milk and water. Many infants are killed each year by bringing them to the table with the family and giving them a little bit of this, that, and the other,

CUTICURA BABY

for which the little stomach is not fitted. Wait till baby gets its teeth before you put food into its mouth all that needs to be chewed. They are killed just as surely, though not so quickly, as if they had been fed poison. When a baby dies they always give it the name of diarrhea, cholera or summer complaint, convulsions, or brain fever. These are just some of the names for the result of poisoning with unfit food. The rubber-tube bottle is a device of the "evil one" for lazy mothers.

Great care must be taken that children are not fed with milk that has been turned by a thunder-storm.

⚮ ⚮ ⚮ ⚮

If baby looks into a broken looking glass, it will have crooked teeth.

No Patent Medicines

Have nothing to do with quack or patent medicines. It is generally recognized that the handsomer the man the better quack he makes. The family physician is a great blessing, more so than his medicine. Never fail to send for him in time, if the disease proves stubborn; but let him understand that you wish advice, not his medicine. When a doctor leaves he feels he has to leave medicine whether necessary or not. But as your child grows, you will gain confidence in nature that will be a great rock of defense, mother nature will never disappoint you.

Air Baby Daily

The family circle is where children learn their earliest lessons in vice or virtue. To be lax in moral, or religious teachings they soon acquire bad habits and principles from impure associations. See that their playmates, books and toys are carefully selected. They do love their tops, marbles and yarn dolls.

Baby should be taken for an airing each day in the carriage, and it won't hurt the pale, nervous mother to catch a breath likewise.

ℐ ℐ ℛ ℛ

Mothers must be careful not to give her broom time that belongs to the children.

ℐ ℐ ℛ ℛ

Let the children get dirt upon themselves; earth is very much akin to us all, and soils them not inwardly. Fear not they make acquaintance with the pigs, donkeys and chickens; they may form worse friendships with wiser looking ones.

Mother's Kiss Will Do Wonders

Sauerkraut taken fresh from the tub makes an excellent poultice for hurts, burns and such accidents, but a mother's kiss will also do wonders.

Nine out of ten children who die of croup might have been saved by the timely application of roast onions, mashed and laid upon a folded napkin, and goose oil, sweet oil or lard poured warm to the throat and upper part of chest, feet and hands.

For colds, hoarseness, or indications of croup, slice raw onion, sprinkled with sugar, let stand until the juice is extracted, pour off the juice and give a tea-spoonful every hour, oftener if case is severe.

A daily evacuation of the bowels in children at a certain hour each day will remain through-out life, except when interfered with by sickness or failing powers which are often a consequent upon old age and at that time a bit of rhubarb will regulate.

Greasing navel, bowels and up and down the spine at night before going to bed promotes regular action of the bowels and cures constipation.

For Sore Throat: Salt Pork and Raw Onions

For a severe cold, keep the bowels open with castor oil, grease the throat, breast and back with pig's feet oil, goose grease, lard or smoked ham rinds, or the frying of salt pork or bacon. For sore throat, chop fat salt pork and raw onions together, put them in a sack and tie around the throat. Leave on until the throat is entirely well.

Going "barefoot" is a very common practice. Where do you suppose blood diseases begin? The serious effects do not manifest themselves immediately but will produce problems and disease when it is least expected.

Jumping the rope is an injurious and dangerous amusement, often resulting in disease of the spine or brain.

Eating of snow, except in very limited quantities, producing catarrh, congestion and other troubles, can be avoided.

Feather pillows are death to children. Make them of straw or hair and not too large.

The juvenile feat of standing on the head has injurious effects. Blood appears to gush out of their eyes and cheeks. It congests the brain and is injurious to the optic nerve and impairs the circulation. So, why let them do it!

ℐ ℐ ℘ ℘

Have the children dress by the stove on chilly mornings and on chilly evenings either wrap hot irons in a towel or a warming pan with hotcoals and stick them between their ice-cold sheets.

ℐ ℐ ℘ ℘

A child's hair should be kept short until ten years old, whether boy or girl.

Be Loving and Patient

In the hot season, children should be kept out of the sun after ten o'clock, and may sit up later than usual at night to enjoy the cool evenings.

Tax your nerves to bear with noise and don't worry so much about "mussing things." Coax them to read aloud to you, while your weary

needle drives in and out of its endless darning. Be loving and patient, your reward will surely come.

Taffy, stick candy, gumdrops, penny candies, all-day suckers, licorice whips, peppermint drops, ginger drops, lemon drops, bonbons, and sugar plums are all fatal poisons concealed in pretty confectionery. The coloring used often is lead, mercury, copper, or arsenic. Little by little it poisons the wee folks.

Be certain the children always bow or courtsey in public, how they behave at home is your own concern.

The evils of spanking are grave. They can be serious when given to the spine or the cuffing of the brain, switching is safer and better than to spare the rod and spoil the child.

If their love for you does not suffice to induce them to do your bidding, the fault is yours, not theirs.

Listen to children, do not interrupt, answer them as sincerely and as respectfully as if they were grown up. What they have to say is far better to listen to than most morning callers.

The medium through which the young are to be taught their dependence upon Heaven and their duty toward God and men should consist of green fields, fruits and flowers, sunlit skies, running brooks, balmy winds, the song of the birds, the changing seasons and the summer woods.

Train Your Sons

Mothers, you must train your sons to do such as sew on their own shoe-buttons, properly air a bed, and so forth, so when the boy marries, his wife will be grateful to his wise mother whose thoughtful care saves her many an extra foot-step. In case of illness, such a man will not be the helpless clumsy creature that so often rasps his poor wife's over-wrought nerves, but a helpful skillful nurse.

Your Daughter

Your sons may love, honor and revere you, but as the years go on it is your daughter who is closest to you, your woman child. Make her girlhood a happy one so a good seed will be planted, and from generation to generation the good that you have done will grow like the beautiful green vine until it covers all of the house of life.

Teach the Daughter

Teach her how to wear a "calico" dress and do it like a queen.

Teach her to say "No" and mean it, or "Yes" and stick to it.

Teach her that tight lacing is uncomely, as well as very injurious to health.

Teach her to regard morals and habits, and not money, in selecting her associates.

Teach her that a good, steady, church-going farmer, mechanic, clerk or teacher, without a cent is worth more than forty loafers or non-producers in broadcloth.

✎ ✎ ✎ ✎

Mothers, see that the material of your growing daughter's dress is not too tight across the chest. See that this most delicate and sensitive part of her body is always kept cool and well supported. A full bust is hardly admirable in an unmarried girl. One is not fond of over ripe pears.

Always wash the bust with cold water in upward strokes. Never touch them with other than the utmost delicacy as otherwise cancer develops.

It won't be long before the children will be paddling their own canoes and buffeting life's waves.

The True Mother

The care of darling baby is no trouble to a true mother. If, after all is done for them, they seem to you to be growing coarse and unlovely,

smile upon them often, kiss them, caress them. Don't let the pressing duties of the younger ones lead you to neglect the older ones. If a child once learns to do without mother's caresses, you can never again make them necessary to that child.

In conclusion, the mother who worries should fight this bad habit as though it was a physical enemy. Bear the troubles of the day bravely and do not borrow those of tomorrow. In climbing a mountain we sometimes come to what looks like a wall of rock, look closer and we see a narrow path to see us to safety. Always look for a path, there is always a way.

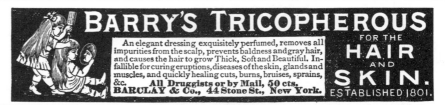

Reading, 'Ritin' & 'Rithmetic

Let Nature Wake Up Children

If children who attend school are puny, take them away from the school whether at the head or tail of the class. See that the children learn deportment, the rules of arithmetic, to spell correctly, to write a plain hand, and to punctuate their sentences. Teach them to never dress beyond their means, never spend their last dollar, unless for food to keep themselves or someone else from starving. Advise them always to keep a little money in their pocket, and if they can scrape together five dollars, they should put it in a savings bank. It will serve as a magnet to attract other money that might be foolishly spent. As soon as they can command the means, they should buy a piece of ground. One should never be afraid to go in debt for land, for it increases in value.

To save is absolutely the only way to amass a solid fortune. Fortunes do not come by chance. Fortune is for those who, by diligence, honesty and frugality place themselves in a position to grasp the boon. The best evidence is a yearly deposit in a savings bank.

One must learn to estimate properly the value of what is called leisure time. There is entirely too much of this in the world. Rest is necessary and play is well in its place, but young men who hope to do something in life must not expect to play one-third of their time. They must burn the mid-night oil.

To Learn Principles Thoroughly Is to Succeed

One should never consider time wasted that is spent in learning rudiments. In acquiring a knowledge of any art or handicraft the greatest difficulty is experienced at the beginning, because our work then possesses little or nothing of interest. The temptation is to skip a few pages at the beginning of a learning book, but such a course is fatal to success. To learn principles thoroughly is to succeed. Be content to learn one thing at a time; whatever you learn, learn it absolutely, without possible question. Step by step, year after year, you will wonder how you outdistanced the geniuses who once seemed so far in advance of you. Valuable knowledge is acquired only by intense devotion. With enough devotion one may even become President of the United States with a salary of $50,000.00 per year!

Never Be Afraid to Say "No"

The schoolmaster or schoolmarm may fail to do so, so you must teach your sons that in order to become a business man, they must attend only to business matters during business hours. In the office, act like a business man, do not run through the halls and in stopping, slide across the terrazzo floors, throw waste paper, cigar and cigarette stubs and

remnants of lunch out the windows, shoot rubber bands or paper fasteners at one another or be of boisterous conduct on pay-day.

Social calls are best adapted to the social circle. Business can be made known in a few words. Dealings with a stranger must be carefully considered, and tried friendship duly appreciated. A mean act will soon recoil and a man of honor will be esteemed. Leave "tricks of the trade" to those whose education was never completed. Treat all with respect, confide in few, wrong no man. Never be afraid to say "No," or rectify a wrong. Leave nothing for tomorrow that should be done today. Trust no man's appearances; they are often deceptive. Rogues generally dress well. The rich are generally plain. Be well satisfied before you give credit that to whom you give are safe and to be trusted.

When a man begins to dream of his work, he is under too great mental strain.

The old proverb that all things come to him who waits is a pretty and pleasant theory, but nothing comes to anyone who waits and does no more. There is nothing in the world of any value that has not to be struggled for and those who sit down and fold their hands expecting fate and fortune to bring them what they most desire, will meet with the disappointment they deserve. That which is worth having is worth working for, but the waiting is the hardest struggle of an impatient spirit.

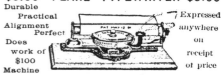

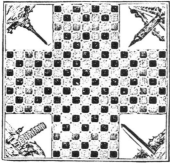

Learn to Play Cards

Though a man may take no great pleasure in card-playing, it is very desirable that he should learn those games that are most played in society, whist and euchre for example. If a fourth hand is wanted at a rubber, he should be able to not only take it, but to acquit himself fairly well. To cheat is to be guilty of a species of buffoonery. A man must forgo playing if he has a temper, as it is necessary to bear ill-luck with composure. In good society one must remember to play with money and not for money. Lotteries make men discontented, idle and vicious.

Profanity is more or less a profession of your loyalty to the devil. Save your breath to cool your porridge.

Tell this to your young man: If another man threatens to do you bodily harm, ask him if he is in earnest. If he says he is, RUN. There is more glory in avoiding a melee by running away, if he has never struck any one he should hardly know how to go to work to do it, but if cornered, he should teach him, to the best of his ability.

Put on your thinking cap, education begins the gentleman; but reading, good company, and reflection must finish him. Do not deny the existence of Him to whom millions of years are but a moment, and millions of miles but a point.

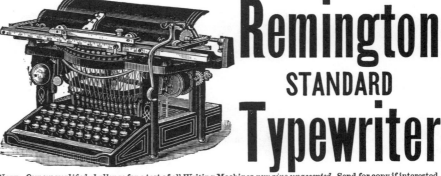

Dress Making

Protection, then Beauty

The first object of dress is the protection of the body, second to enhance and bring out the beauty. To be in correct taste, it must be "becoming," and in this sense dressing is an art worth the attention and study of the most intellectual and accomplished woman. The beauty of the eye, does not lie in its money value. Any simpleton in petticoats, who has plenty of money, can order the clothes in the latest Paris styles, but some quiet woman with brains and taste will be sure to outshine her in "society." Low-necked dresses, dragging skirts, corsets and stays, paddings, heavy shirts which rest on the hips, heavy veils, high-heeled boots and every other unphysiological abomination in dress, mars beauty and destroys health. Tight-lacing, it is whispered, is for the weak-minded.

Mind the Purse; Mend the Clothes

With the stern fact of a slender purse to be kept in mind, the humble fabrics can be used to work miracles with patience, practice and study of one's own figure to bring out its good points. Every rip and rent should receive attention as soon as it occurs. It is commendable to work over old clothes as, "One a charm from dress can borrow."

One can be absolutely fetching in a pink calico sun-bonnet with

39

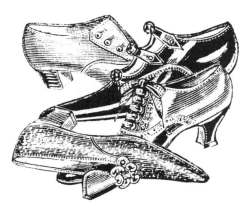

tiny pink rose-buds, but black is handsome, lady-like and irreproachable. She who is not the fortunate possessor of one good black dress is really worthy of pity.

Men have been heard to say that women never brush their dresses. However untrue that sweeping assertion may be, it is certain that too little attention is paid to freeing dresses from the dust of the house and soil of the street.

Shoes pay for good care. On taking them off do not leave them in the shape of the foot, but smooth them by stretching out the wrinkles and bending the soles straight. If buttons are lacking, sew them on immediately; never wear a shoe with a single button off, as it destroys the shape. To cure a squeaking boot, drive a peg into the middle of the sole.

Straight tears in underwear may be mended in the same manner as sheets, but when parts are worn thin, cotton, silk or woolen drawers may be darned the same as table linen.

Trowsers as Long as His Father's

Very few grown people understand the hardship it is to little folks to wear outgrown, clumsy or ill-fitting garments. They are quite alive to the mortification of wearing shabby or ill-cut and ill-made coats and trowsers.

For boys, small pantaloons are readily cut from larger ones, and even where the latter are seriously impaired, it is still possible to make good new ones out of them. If the back is in holes, the thin part can be

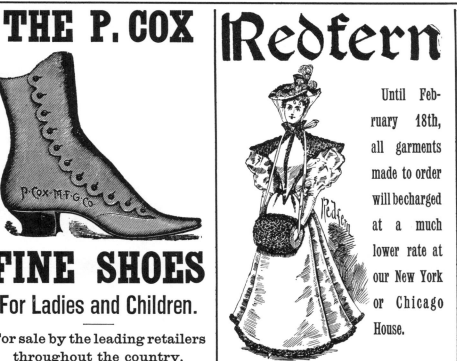

replaced by long gore-shaped pieces. In cutting fronts, try not to have the exact spot come at the knee that came there before. The fly should be lined with strong drilling interlines with canvas to give sufficient support for the button-holes. Short knee breeches are easy to make but, after a certain age, all the king's horses and all the king's men would be a force insufficient to compel a little boy to give up his inalienable right to have his trowsers as long as his father's.

To Dress Little Girls

It is cruel to condemn a dainty little maid, with naturally dainty tastes and love for pretty things to wear ugly, ill-fashioned clothes.

Young people sometimes feel that it makes very little difference how mothers and grand-mothers dress as long as they them-selves can make as fair a show as the family circumstances allow. It is disgraceful, but still hanging about the country—a purely American notion—that a young lady, even if her parents are not rich, must be gaily and richly clothed, and be able to show soft jeweled hands, as white as the piano keys she touches deftly or otherwise, as the case may be, while mamma spends her over-worked time in the meanest of clothes, and by reason of shabbiness is seldom seen by her daughter's friends, or by any one else except at church. Too often it is conscience rather than choice that takes her there, where the comfort of the service is swallowed in the conscious-ness of the utter forlornness and awkwardness of her appearance in obsolete dress and antiquated mantilla that were bought long before the daughters grew up to monopolize what little comfort and luxury life in narrow circumstances can give.

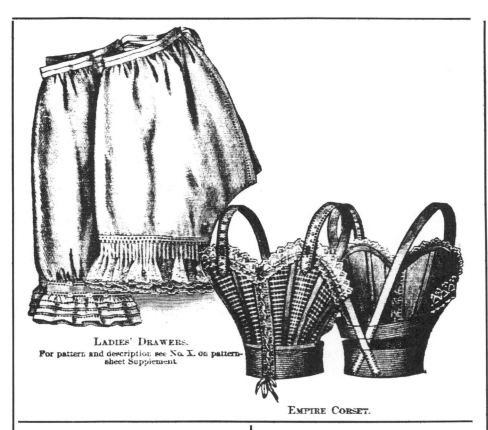

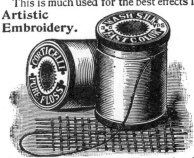

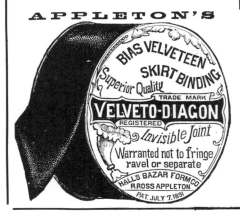

Caps for an Old Lady Should Be Pure White

The grand-mother, whose failing strength takes her partially out of the active cares of life and household, should not be a poor, pushed-aside, forlorn object, to be kept out of sight. The ideal dress for an old lady is severely plain velvet, with soft tulle handkerchief folded across the breast, rich lace ruffles at the wrist to shade the withered hands, and a decorous cap, which makes no attempt to be a head-dress, but has protecting strings of lace or ribbon to tie loosely under the chin. We can not all dress our dear old grand-mothers, thus grandly and picturesquely, but remember, that the love of pretty things to wear begins with a woman's life and generally lasts as long as she does.

If the old lady is very stout and likes the style, a single-skirted dress is becoming.

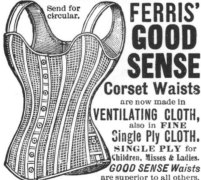
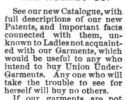

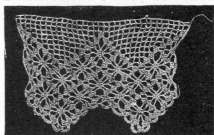

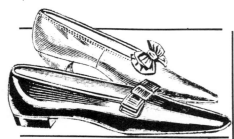

Caps for an old lady should be pure white and bonnets black. Small bonnets are out of the question for old ladies who need a shape that will amply protect the head as well as the back of the neck where there are so many nerve centers that embrace the slightest exposure to ache remorselessly. Still, the bonnet must not be too large, unless to shade a large fat face. A small head and delicate features in a great coal-scuttle of a hat look like a caricature. The beauty of a bonnet lies in its fitness.

When your sewing machine runs heavily, soak it with gasoline or kerosene, wipe dry and oil.

To make rag rugs, cut rags and sew hit or miss, or fancy-striped as you choose. Use wooden needles, round, smooth and pointed at one end, of any convenient length. The knitting is done back and forth (like suspenders) always take off the first stitch.

The everyday darning, mending, making patchwork quilts with scraps and your beautiful embroidery can be such a delight when shared with neighbors in the daytime. Always bring your workbasket full to show off your handiwork, share ideas mingled with a little gossip and good cheer which makes the sewing bee a festivity.

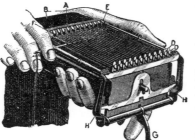

The Management of Help

The Mistress Must Know

The model house should not be large, nor too fine and pretentious for daily use. A family of four or five needs but one maid. However, a young mistress of many a fine mansion should understand house-hold duties because servants are quick to note the ignorance of the mistress.

A mistress who begins to think herself superior should take a turn in the kitchen for a day or two. Often it will be a revelation to her.

As a maid, you must speak only when spoken to, obey the mistress, don't eat too much, don't keep asking for more money, and be watchful of your temper and your tongue.

As mistress you must put yourself in the "girl's" place, and apply the "golden rule" in all dealings with her. She must recognize the fact that character, and not station or wealth, makes the lady, and that it is possible for those who serve to respect themselves. You must let your domestics see that you do not consider their work degrading, but honorable. Above all, never show them, by word, look or action, that you "look down" on them because of their work. Unless the "girl" is vain, lazy, slovenly, or dishonest, whoever looks down on her because she does honest work conscientiously and well, is a fool, and not worth minding.

In all families whose style of living demands help in the house-hold duties, the management of servants is the great American puzzle. "Girls"

come and go like the seasons, sometimes with the weeks. The one who is "such a treasure" today, packs her trunk and leaves her mistress in the lurch tomorrow, or, if she happens to have a conscience and works on faithfully, she becomes the mistress and runs the house-hold in her own way. Her employer lives in mortal fear of offending and losing her. This state of things is due partly to the fact that all girls who go out to service, do so as a make-shift until they marry or obtain some more congenial work. Another cause is the fact that too many American women, who ought to know better, regard work as degrading, instead of positively elevating and ennobling when it is well and conscientiously done.

You, as house-keeper and mistress, should not be hasty in your dictation of duties to your servants, but firm. The first month is spent in civilizing the girl. If she is of average ability, she should be able to answer the door-bell, dust and sweep a room tolerably well, make coffee, warm up potatoes and possibly be trusted to fix breakfast alone by the second month. By the third month, one should be able to breathe more freely; however, by the fourth month, she believes she knows it all and demands an increase in wages. It seems one must pay ten dollars a month for the privilege of teaching an ignorant creature the trade which is to gain her livelihood, and the moment she begins to be of the least use, she wants double for what we have taught her. Sister House-keepers! We are to blame. The reform must begin at home. We must stop paying first-class wages for third-class work.

House-
Keeping

Insane Asylums Are Full of House-Keepers

When mother nature summons the stirring winds to help clear away the dead leaves and winter litter for the coming grass and flowers, every house-keeper has a feeling of sympathy, and begins to talk of house-cleaning. The first bright sunshine of spring reveals unsuspected dust and cobwebs, and to her imagination even the scrubbing-brushes and brooms seems anxious to begin the campaign.

Most women, after constant confinement during the winter months, are more or less run down in the spring, and the change from the bracing temperatures of winter to the enervating warmth of the first spring days is likely to result in a lowering of tone that may expose them to serious mischief from over-exertion. For these reasons there is a gradual change of sentiment in favor of making spring house-cleaning a simple affair, put off the heavy work until fall.

Keep Calm, Cook, Serve
and Send Out Rays of Sunshine

At breakfast, as always happens, women must serve everything and pour the coffee besides. The best any woman can do is keep calm, cook and serve healthful and plain food, sending out rays of sunshine, forgetting herself until every-one else is ready. After this, if she be wise, she will eat her own breakfast slowly, resting body and mind, for the work of the day.

Then, clear the table, soak dishes soiled with mush, milk or eggs, and put silver in pitcher of warm water.

Leave the bed-room to air and sun to shine while you return to the kitchen to wash the dishes; making certain they are put away at once. Return to bed-room, empty the chamber pots and wash and wipe the bed-room toilet china.

Prepare the luncheon. After the dishes are washed, clean the kitchen, bathe and change clothes, rest thoroughly, replenish fire.

Then it's time to make the soap and candles, pump and haul the water (remembering that nearly every drop that is carried in has to be carried out again). Fish need to be scaled, chickens have to be fed, and the fat ones butchered, then plucked and roasted, butter churned, eggs gathered, herbs dried, a gunny-sack of grain lugged from here to there and back again, yeast made and so on. Stir, grind, sweep, knead, sort, soak, rub, dip, turn, wring, hang, shake, fold, sprinkle—always remembering to account to God for every single wasted hour.

Cleaning House

The melancholy days that come,
    The saddest of the year,
When scrubbing-brushes, mops, and brooms
    Are flying far and near,—
When carpets, curtains, rugs, and beds
    Are stretched on fence and line,
And everything is upside down—
    O, sad, unhappy time.

Don't get your bowels in an uproar and upset your house-hold by cleaning it all at once as it will drive your husband to distraction and the children to the neighbors. Use a little womanly tact, and clean one or two rooms at a time. If you are a lone woman you will need the help of a stout girl.

The insane asylums are full of house-keepers just at the middle of life and usually of limited means; they have taken more upon themselves and endured too much. One who gives her whole body to scrubbing, scouring, setting to rights, darning, piecing, pinching, procuring, ornamenting, furbishing, studying and preparing recipes, up early in the morning and to bed late at night, is not a good house-keeper as she wears down her own existence to death or insanity in pursuit of it. A house-keeper has not only a body, she has a soul. It is her duty to make her house-hold life simple enough to allow herself time to read and look about her and give her family attention other than material comforts.

Old Underwear Is Useful

Good house-keeping means plenty of matches in every room. It is most wretched to hunt all over the house for a match. It is a good idea to give one daughter the duty of seeing that all match boxes are always filled.

From the time of the cock's crow till the cows come home, make the most of your brain and eyes, and let no one dare tell you that you are devoting yourself to a low sphere of action. Keep cool and self-possessed. Work done quietly about the house seems easier. When the kitchen is reached by the attacking party, a slamming of oven doors, and the rattle and clatter of dishes, tire and bewilder everybody about the house. Those who accomplish much in house-keeping, and the same is true of every other walk in life, are the quiet workers.

Have nothing in your house that you do not know to be useful or believe to be beautiful. Wastefulness is evidence of a lack of brain and culture. Rags can be made into carpet rugs or sold to the ragman. Old stockings may be turned into a quilt. Old underwear is useful for dusters. Consider discarded articles to see if they can be given away, sold or used for fuel, if not, throw them together to make a bonfire to celebrate with when the house-cleaning is finished.

Save yourself whenever you can, sit down whenever you can. Sit down to prepare vegetables, sit down to wash dishes, sit down to the ironing-board. There is enough in life that has to be done, without vexing our souls and wearing out our bodies over work that is not essential to our happiness and well-being.

Whatever may be the opinion of the butterflies of the period, house-keeping is an accomplishment in comparison to which, all others are trivial. It comprehends all that goes to make up a well-ordered home, where the sweetest relations rest on a firm foundation, and the purest sentiments thrive. If girls were taught to take as much genuine pride in dusting a room well, hanging a curtain gracefully, or broiling a steak to a nicety, as they feel when they have mastered one of Mozart's or

Beethoven's grand symphonies, there would be fewer complaining husbands and unhappy wives.

ℐ ℐ ℕ ℕ

Every woman has just so much time, nobody has any more than twenty-four hours a day. That's all there is, six working days a week; that's all you get unless you steal from Sunday, and if you have to do that, it is better to postpone until next week. Anything that sticks over the end of the year, saw off and put in the stove.

ℐ ℐ ℕ ℕ

Few people die from over-work. Many lose their good looks from idleness and sulkiness. It is better to wear out than to rust out.

The Cellar

On Monday, be up early and take a man to the cellar. The cellar should be the first order of the day, or else it is left to the last, when you are tired, and then you just give it a "lick and a promise." Do it while you are strong. Do not work so hard as to make yourself sick; better a little dirty than to have a spell of sickness.

First inspect, then sweep the cellar walls, ceiling, and what have you. Let the dust settle, then sweep again. Wash the cellar stairs. If one is so fortunate as to have a furnace, wash the coal bins and white wash the walls of the cellar. If there is time left-over, run upstairs and clean the china-closet, kitchen closets and pantry.

ℐ ℐ ℕ ℕ

Every part of the house, from attic to cellar is under the house-keeper's charge. The first duty of the day is to make the kitchen fire; take up and sift the ashes, brush all dust from the range, wash the stove and polish with blacking. Rinse out the tea-kettle, add water and place on fire, sweep and dust the kitchen and put the breakfast dishes on to heat.

Put all rooms in order, dust the front hall, sweep painted floors with a hairbrush, after the dirt is up, go over with old flannel on the brush to get the dust. Air and brush the dining-room then draw the shades. Collect the lamps and trim them. Sweep and wash the sidewalk, if you live in the city. It is best to get this done before there are any passers-by. Do not wash in freezing weather as it would be dangerous to limb and life. At last when we have passed over the river there will be no more toil, no more tears, no more sickness!

The Bed-Room

The Head of the Bed Should Face North

The family bed-room should be on the first floor if possible, if the house is properly built and there is no dampness. The room should be plain, and warm, with the furniture simple and scanty; chairs free from stuffing so they won't hold dust. Just an easy chair and extra clothing for the bed outranks the luxury of elegant homes with their lovely embroideries, dainty toilette cushions and various knickknacks which please the eye but are of no use. Half a muslin curtain is enough and keep all clothing not in use out of the room. The bed-room need not have any decorations or pictures as this room is made to sleep in and not to lie awake in. Always see that the head of the bed is facing north as the human body's head must be in this direction in order to preserve the harmonious circulation of the nervo-electric fluids.

Iron or brass beds are more sanitary and inners husks of corn or oat straw make an excellent under-bed. Hair is the best and cheapest. Spanish moss soon mats down. Feather beds are soft and warm but do injury. They make us nervous. They weaken and impair our every vital function. They retain the dampness of perspiration, and thus we develop germs of disease. The odor is very offensive and unwholesome. If you have one, put it in a spare room, lock the door, and lose the key.

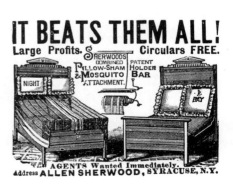

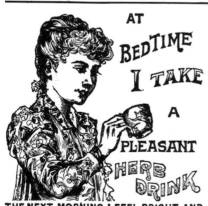
The bed of the guest chamber should stand so that when one opens the eyes in the morning the light from the window will be directly upon them. Chambers should always be provided with transoms over the doors. Have two crocheted pockets tacked on wash-stand doors for bathing sponges and rough towels to make the morning bath such a luxury.

If you are not in bed by ten o'clock, health and eyesight will fail.

Upon retiring, keep the body warm, but throw open the window; let the winds of Heaven have free play. In freezing winter-time go to bed in a hurry. First undress by a good fire, warm and dry the feet well, draw on the stockings again, run into the bed-room, jump into bed, bundle up, with head and ears under cover for a minute or more, then uncover your head, next draw off your stockings, straighten out, turn on your right side and go to sleep. Only an invalid sleeps in the same room with a fire.

Sleeping in the Barn Is Conducive to Sleep

Sleeplessness is the loss of power to cast off the burdens of the day, caused by nervousness and too much mental work, especially at night, to be able to find rest. This is one of the greatest personal afflictions; yet, wakefulness at night is an acquired habit, The best remedy is to get away from excitement, drink hop tea or get a hop pillow to sleep on. Sleeping in the barn on the hay is often conducive to sleep. Do not talk politics or religion when you can avoid it, and recite poetry or the multiplication tables upon retiring.

As soon as you put your head on the pillow is the time to plan for the next day's work. "Method and habit" are two little fairies that will help you make your work disappear.

Do not indulge in sensual or intemperate habits if you have asthma. Sleep on a hard mattress, and frequently take the country air.

Early rising is one of the secrets of successful management, but never get out of bed on the left side; it is unlucky. Spring out of bed, dash the feet with cold water, wipe dry, return to bed and remain there until they are once again warm.

Bright, wide awake women look at their tongues every morning: If it be furred, the stomach or bowels are out of order. You must resort to cathartics and abstinence till the tongue is clean.

The best cure for a night-mare is a physic to cleanse the bowels and then go to bed supperless.

The modern dame is waked by noon,
Some authors say not quite so soon,
Because though sore against her will,
She sat all night up at quadrille.

Don't Make Up Beds Too Soon

In the morning the beds are almost always made up too early. The thrifty house-keeper likes to have rooms put to right in the morning, but it brings up the old adage: "the white glove which hides a dirty hand." The bed should lie open to air, and if possible sunshine, several hours each morning.

While the chamber windows are wide open, take clothes from the beds and spread over the chairs or a low screen so the air may pass through freely. Only on a fair day should you clean your mattress by taking it into an empty room and removing the hair slowly, so that you won't get choked with dust. Pick the hair over thoroughly and wash a bit at a time, use several pails of strong soap-suds. Rinse and dry as much as possible and lay between two thin sheets of muslin, basting them together at the ends and tacking here and there, then hang up to dry.

Sprinkle Lavender to Drive Off Fleas

Beat pillows and bolsters and place in a current of air. If it is necessary to clean feather pillows, place them on a plot of clean green grass during a heavy rain storm. When thoroughly wet, hang in shady place where you know the sun will never peep.

Make the beds using a good quality cotton cloth sheet that you have your-self made, as the cloth costs only 25 cents, and the already made ones cost one dollar; it is only common sense to make one's own. Cover the bedstead as well as the bed with the dust cloth during the day so the dirt won't lodge in grooves and carvings.

By cleaning all bed-room ware and marble top wash-stands and tables with a rag dipped in turpentine, you will not only clean but disinfect as well.

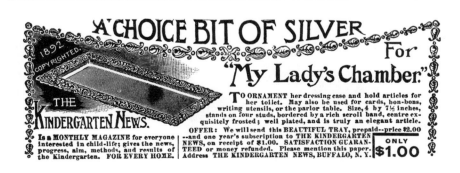

Put away trimmings of rose geraniums and sweet clover in envelopes in drawers, especially with your handkerchiefs.

Sprinkle a few drops of oil of lavender about the bed to drive off fleas. Every July or August examine the beds for bed bugs. If found, use gasoline or lamp-oil where ever they are found, it will not injure floor or carpet.

To clean looking-glass, use warm rain-water with just enough spirits of ammonia to make it slippery. Dry with the tissue paper you have been saving for this purpose.

The best oil lamps are the safest and cheapest. Student lamps are the least trying to the eyes. Every household must have at least one of these which range in price from two dollars to fifteen or more. If the price is over eight dollars, it is owing to metal and ornamentation not quality of light. Each morning the lamp must be filled with oil, the wick trimmed and the shade and chimney cleaned.

Run a feather dipped in oil on hinges to prevent creaking.

The best way to cool a bedroom in summer is to wet a large cloth and suspend it over a line where, if possible, a draught will strike it. This will cool the air by evaporation approximately ten degrees according to circumstances. This plan is frequently practiced in hot climates.

The sewing room should be as remote from the sleeping and sitting rooms as possible; the attic is nice.

The Parlour

Nail the Rugs Down

The sitting room is the most important room in the house. Horse-hair sofas and other furniture should be selected for comfort with broad seats, and not for show, and should be low for women and children. See that the couch has plenty of pillows. There should be a firm table of good size, a book case, a Japanese vase and, if possible an open fire. The appointments should be brass. On your ebony piano with a cream color scarf with rich embroidery the family photos should top. On the walls should be many pictures that suggest pleasant things, full of life and color. Scattered throughout should be a few thrifty ferns, or perhaps a begonia, wandering Jew, Coleus, Star of Bethlehem or evergreens, and think about a vase which holds a cluster of carnations. There should be doilies aplenty scattered about.

Light is as needful to health as fresh air. Take a plant and put it in your dark cellar, and it will be sickly in a short time. So it is with human beings. Spirits of lavender on a lump of salt ammonia make the air fragrant.

Be a plucky wife, not a frowzy one, move furniture around periodically to give a welcome change to all but the husband who will growl awhile, but he will get used to it.

Using Mamma's Christmas Gift

Your parlour needs a woman's touch, it looks well painted cream and yellow, electric blue or dainty old rose. A floor painted yellow ochre is nice. An Oriental rug on the floor looks well, but be certain there are no carpet tacks to step on as a rusty tack is dangerous business.

A home-made carpet can easily be made: Paste the floor of the room over with newspapers. Over this paste wall-paper of a pattern to look like carpet or oil-cloth. Put down as smoothly as possible. Use a good flour paste. Then size and varnish it. Dark glue and common furniture varnish may be used. Best to nail the rugs down.

The front hall should have a French plate mirror; an inexpensive blue and white or terra cotta Japanese umbrella jar is indispensable. A hatstand and a large photograph not of any sentiment in a plain wood frame.

Soot upon the Carpet

Even with husk mats and foot-scrapers, a thorough sweeping once or twice a week is necessary for the tidiest of house-keepers. There is more art in sweeping a carpet than a novice is apt to suppose. It calls for skill and intelligence. Before the sweeping commences, open blinds and let in light, open windows if not stormy. Then scatter the carpet over with saw-dust, moistened bran, salt, damp coffee-grounds, tea leaves, or moist earth. Should soot fall upon the carpet, cover it with dry salt and it may be swept up without leaving smears.

In sweeping, an old broom should never be used, and a new one should be kept especially for the carpets. Clear one corner of settee or other furniture and begin sweeping toward the center with short light strokes, careful not to raise the dust. The second time over use more force. For smaller, easier to handle carpets, lay on the grass or hang on the clothes-line and beat on the wrong side with a cane.

Clean corners with a sharp-pointed stick. The wings of fowls, such as turkeys, geese and chickens are useful to dig out the corners in washing windows. Do not leave them where the cat can chew them.

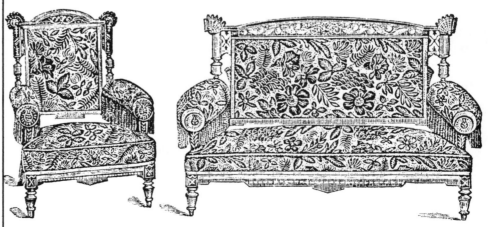

Furniture should have broad seats and be low for children and women.

Moving the Dust from One Place to Another

Dust is defined as "earth or other matter in fine dry particles so attenuated that it can be raised and carried by the wind." Some well-meaning ladies use a feather duster to brush down all tapestry, picture cords, frames and curtains. However, the old-fashioned feather duster is useful for moving the dust from one place to another, but for no other purpose.

To dust correctly, spread the cloth out and gather dust into it, folding it in as you work. Shake it out the window.

To clean a papered wall, cut into eight pieces, a large loaf of bread, two days old. Blow dust off wall with a bellows, rub down a piece of the bread, in half yard strokes, beginning at the top of the room, until upper part is cleaned, then go round again repeating until all has been gone over. If grease spots appear, put blotting paper over spots and press with a hot flat-iron.

Cold tea is good for washing wood-work. Do not slop water enough about to run a mill, for it can be done just as well without making any slop.

Furniture should be dusted with an old silk duster. Leather furniture should be washed with a soft cloth wrung out of hot milk. The horse-hair sofa should be cleaned with naphtha. In cleaning windows, crumpled newspapers answer very well.

Furniture Polish

1 Tablespoon sweet oil   1 Tablespoon corn starch
1 Tablespoon lemon juice

"It won't rub off."

Send for Alabastine Rock for Souvenir; also Tint Card.

Blow Cayenne Pepper into Every Crack

To rid your house of moths, take common lamp-oil and wash the floor all over. It smells "loud" but will all be gone in about two days, and so will the moths. Also, when the floor is dry blow cayenne pepper into every crack and crevice, using a small pair of bellows for the purpose. To prevent moths under carpets, grind black pepper and mix with camphor-gum and put thickly under the edges. Snow sprinkled on and swept off before it melts is nice for soiled carpet.

Flies pester every decent respectable citizen. To keep them off gilt frames, boil three or four onions in a pint of water and apply with a soft brush.

Scatter branches of sweet-fern whenever red ants congregate.

To rid the home of mosquitoes, burn gunpowder on a plate with a composition of one part salt petre, intimately mixed with seven parts flower of sulphur. If this doesn't kill them it will drive them away.

In summer use mosquito netting in the windows to keep flies out, or make bags of mosquito netting and fill with sweet clover and hang about the room. Flies are said to abhor sweet clover and geraniums, why not more flowers and fewer flies?

Don't Take the Stove Out Too Soon

Fireplaces roast the front, and freeze the rear of those who don't keep a proper distance, but the snug and cheerful fireside is preferable to all kinds of stoves.

Do not remove stove before the middle of May because if it should get cold in a fire-less room, the children will become unmanageable and husband growls.

Always straighten up the parlour before retiring, and leave the Blessed Book, late papers, magazines, a volume of poetry, or a stereoscope with views for callers.

While painting keep the room well ventilated and eat acid fruits. After house-cleaning is done, paint the kitchen floor. Any woman with a mechanical turn of mind can paint.

The Wash Day

All Good House-Keepers Wash on Monday!

Good soap, rain-water and elbow grease is all that is needed on washday. It really need not be such a bugbear.

Saturday night one must prepare the Monday morning wash water. Rain-water is the best, but is the old-fashioned programme for washing. Use good soft water if it can be had. If not, soften a barrel-full of well-water by pouring into it water in which half a peck or more of hard-wood ashes have been boiled, together with the ashes themselves. When enough has been added as to produce the desired effect, the water takes on a curdled appearance, and soon settles perfectly clear. If milky, more ashes and lye must be added as before, care being taken not to add too much, or it will affect the hands unpleasantly. On the other hand, if too little is put in, the clothes will turn yellow.

$$\mathscr{D} \quad \mathscr{D} \quad \mathscr{D} \quad \mathscr{D}$$

Gather up all clothes which are ready, and the rest as they are taken off. Spread a white sheet on the floor and empty the contents from the laundry bags. Sort, with all table linen and doilies in one pile, the bed and body linen in another, coloured clothes, hosiery and coarser articles in a third. Flannels and woolens by themselves.

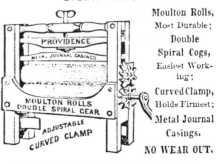
63

List of utensils you will need: Boiler, wringer, wash-board, three or four tubs, two or three pails, clothes stick and dipper. Wooden tubs and pails are most common, but those of paper or wood-pulp are lighter and will not fall to pieces if allowed to dry. The wringer may cost five dollars, but will last a long time. It is true economy to buy one with rolls made of pure rubber.

Get It Done by Ten

On Monday morning, build a fire in the backyard to heat the wash water, set tubs so smoke won't blow in the eyes if the wind is strong. Have the water in the tub as warm as the hand will bear. Wash first one boiler full with a handful of borax to about ten gallons of water, which helps to whiten the clothes and is used by the Germans, who are famous for their snowy linen. Extra powder is used for crinolines. Throw a handful of tansy into the boiler. It will make the water green, but will whiten the clothes. Use a corn cob to rub the mud from clothing; use the wash-board when necessary. Rinse in two waters with bluing last. Re-starching is usually necessary for shirtbosoms, wristbands and collars.

Use a broomstick handle to move the clothes from one tub to another. Clothes should be hung on the line by ten o'clock in the morning. White clothing should be hung in the sun and coloured in the shade. Keep starched clothes out of the wind. Be certain to turn clothing right side out and shake thoroughly before hanging! Do not hang by corners. One can be proud to see clothes hung neatly pinned in categories and with esthetic colour patterns on the line. Stockings should be hung in pairs, and men's underwear must not mingle with the ladies' underwear. Spread towels on the grass, hang old rags on the fence, and watch your backyard for dirt and bones.

⌇⌇ ⌇⌇

To clean a silk dress, brush with a velvet brush. Grate two potatoes into a quart of water. Let it stand to settle, then strain it off quite clear. Sponge dress with this potatoe water.

⌇⌇ ⌇⌇

The way to wash silk or thread gloves is to place the gloves on the hands, wash the same as if washing the hands, rinse and dry with a towel. Keep gloves on until half dried. Take off carefully and fold them up so that they will look like new. Lay between clean towels under a weight.

⌇⌇ ⌇⌇

To stiffen linen cuffs and collars, add a small piece of white wax and one tea-spoonful brandy to a pint of fine starch.

⌇⌇ ⌇⌇

Moth millers fill the air with their dusty wings and eat on furs and cloths of all kinds. Beat furs outside with a rubber hose. Fold them tightly in black inky newspapers, or sprinkle with alum. Washing shelves with a solution of corrosive sublimate is said to be a "dead shot."

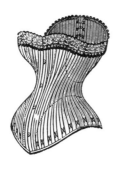

To wash corsets, choose a clear, sunny day. Make a strong solution of soap-suds with a small amount of ammonia. Spread the corsets on a clean board and take and scrub with a good stiff brush. Do not wring out and the shape will not change.

To clean woolen dresses—also silk or velvet—anything except cotton goods, soak and wash them in gasoline. It pays to buy the best gasoline, five gallons at a time.

Ladies who are in mourning suffer much inconvenience from the injury caused by tear drops falling upon their crape, for each drop makes a conspicuous white mark. If before set, these areas are clapped between the hands till dry, no spots will appear.

If you have clothing that smells bad, bury them in the ground for a day or two.

Always Count the Clothes-Pins

Every house-keeper ought to provide a pair of mittens for hanging out the clothes in the winter, or set the clothes-pin bag in a kettle of boiling water. The hot clothes-pins will help to keep the hands warm in freezing weather. Add salt to the rinse water to make the clothes on the line less liable to freeze, or be torn when whipped by the wind, or when being removed from the line. Always count the clothes-pins when gathering them up.

After a woman leaves her wash-tub, where she has become heated from the steam and hot water, and the pores of her arms and hands have opened, do not go bareheaded and barearmed into the chill air to hang clothes. She must remember her health is capital, and that without it, she will become a burden to herself and others. Wear a shawl to protect shoulders and lungs and clean white mittens and rubbers before venturing outdoors.

If the weather is too bad for hanging outside, place hooks or small pulleys on either side of the kitchen, a few inches above the head of the tallest member of the family. Stretch the line back and forth across the room with the heaviest articles nearest the stove, and keep a good warm fire. Open windows a few inches at the top for ventilation. An entire wash for a family, or half a dozen persons can be thus dried without serious inconvenience in an ordinary kitchen. If that idea doesn't appeal to you, hang them in the attic.

ℐ ℐ ℚ ℚ

To wash knitted or crocheted shawls, fold as flat as possible and lay carefully in a pillowcase, run through at intervals with basting thread to keep flat. Put in the oven on a big platter, shaking and turning occasionally.

ℐ ℐ ℚ ℚ

Boil lace curtains in turpentine water, rinse in gum arabic and dip them in tea after the last rinsing to give them an old look.

ℐ ℐ ℚ ℚ

For coloured fabrics, either gelatine or isinglass makes a satisfactory stiffening. Soak one-fourth of an ounce of gelatine or isinglass in half a pint of cold water for one hour. Pour on this one quart of boiling water. Stir until gelatine is dissolved. Strain. First wring articles dry, dip in gelatine, wring and dry, dampen and iron.

ℐ ℐ ℚ ℚ

No woman should be required to wash more than two pairs of blankets in one day, as this is heavy work.

May Is the Best Month for Bleaching

Calicoes, ginghams, chintz and fancy cotton stockings should be soaked in cold water first. Silk hose and ribbons should be soaked in half a gallon of water with as much sugar of lead as will lie on a quarter dollar. For lawn and muslin dresses, take a clear day and it will be little trouble to do several in a few hours. Shave half a pound of common hard soap into a gallon of boiling water. Put dresses into the first tub of suds, rub gently, or rather "souse" it up and down, squeeze it out. Treat them the same in a tub of bran water; rinse, dry again and sprinkle with a whiskbroom. Roll up in a thick cloth while the iron is heating on the stove. Dresses that have faded may be bleached on the grass. This requires a

clean lawn. May is the best month for bleaching, in winter bleach on snow.

◎ ◎ ◎ ◎

To clean men's clothes, hang garments on a line and beat them with a carriage whip or piece of rubber hose. Brush them thoroughly with a

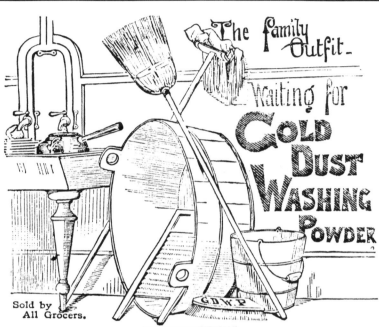

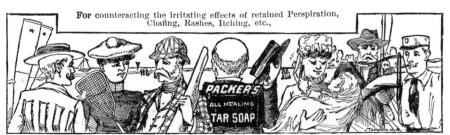

stiff brush, such as horsehair used in the stable for smoothing the coats of horses.

Few gentlemen have the philosophy enough to endure an ill-fitting collar with patience, but not many understand why they do not fit. The fact is, the laundress stretches them the wrong way. She ought to stretch them crosswise, and not lengthwise. It can be done in a twinkling of an eye.

A good husband will eat a cold dinner on washday without mumbling.

Washday Puddin'

Put a layer of bread in a pudding-dish, with little lumps of butter, then a layer of chopped apples with cinnamon and sugar. Then another layer of crumbs and another of apple. So on, till dish is full. Pour over a cup of water and bake till apple is done. Eat with cream and sugar.

When the washing is done, sprinkle all clothes for ironing day. Pour the rinse water on the flower bed and scrub porch with hot soapy water. Turn the tubs upside down.

Go put on a clean dress, smooth hair with side combs and brew a cup of tea. Then go set and rest and rock a spell and count blessings.

Ironing Day

When inviting friends to visits of a week or more, try to fix the time of day for the visit to begin the day after the ironing is done. A girl feels a weight off her mind.

The ironing table should be covered with soft material. An old blanket is excellent with a clean white cotton cover tacked over and pulled so tight that there is not a suggestion of a wrinkle.

The fire must not burn too rapidly. Never let it reach white heat. Keep irons clean and smooth. Whenever the iron gets rough, rub it with salt, wipe it, go over it with beeswax and wipe again. Iron towels first, then sheets, table-clothes, and underwear. Everytime the fire is replenished, handkerchiefs should be ironed.

Arrange flat-irons on the stove in two rows, "heel and toe," so that when you are ready for a hot flat, you can take the next one in order without trying or "sissing" them, being sure of getting the one that has been heated the longest.

Never allow flat-irons to become red hot. Do not keep them on the stove when not in use and never use for cracking nuts or hammering nails. Irons fresh from the fire must be tried on a spare cloth to be certain it isn't hot enough to scorch. When you iron, press hard and do not move in a jerky manner.

To take out scorch, if a shirt-bosom, or any other article that has been scorched in ironing, lay it where the bright sunshine will directly fall on it. Peel and slice two onions, squeeze the juice, and add to half an ounce of fine white soap, cut up two ounces of fuller's earth, and half a pint of vinegar. Boil together. When cool, spread over the scorch, let dry on, then wash.

If your husband's night-shirt is smoothed in front and folded artistically, who is to know whether the back has been ironed or not? I'll venture to say that he will not, unless you tell him. The same with your own night-dresses; and the children's drawers! Little scamps, they soil them in less time than it takes to do them up.

In ironing shirts, a "bosom-board" is indispensable.

Sprinkling your clothes and folding with care and exactness saves ironing. Practice makes perfect.

MRS. POTTS' SAD IRONS
With Forged Stretcher Handle.

Before garments are put away, mend and dry in the air or by a sunny window, then beat with a limber cane. Towards evening, fold them up and lay cut tobacco or cedar chips in their wrinkles, wrap them in newspaper, carefully tie and label them and they are ready for the shelves. Fine dresses and cloaks should be wrapped separately.

Since the sun still rises, since the earth puts forth her blossoms anew, since the bird builds its nest, and the mother smiles at her child, let us have the courage to do what is right and commit the rest to Him who has numbered the stars.

Necessity and Luxury

The Outhouse

This room should be water-tight and be provided in front with a good-fitting door. Always keep the door shut and the window open. The darker this room can be made, the fewer flies will enter. This room should be provided with two or three wire-screened ventilators, as they permit a free circulation of air, and thus not only reduce the odour, but make the outhouse cooler.

Nearly all privies have seats for two persons, but a single privy can be made more economically. Most outhouses are furnished with pages of paper torn from catalogues, but save the soft wrappings found in your peach crates for the comfort of your guests.

At best, the privy is not an attractive addition to the yard. It is possible, however, to reduce its unattractiveness by surrounding it with a lattice-work on which you may train vines or flowers. The fragrant sweet pea or the tall and elegant larkspur are good choices. They add little to the expense, but render the building much less unsightly and much more private.

When you begin to dig for a new outhouse, your first thought should be of its location. Best not too far from the house as it is a long way to shovel when one is in a hurry and the way is blocked by snowdrifts. Also, do not fail to remember that outhouse vaults and wells which connect underground lead to funeral processions.

The Ice House

The place where one finds ice is often the same place of winter amusement, the skating rink. It is a place where we fair damsels go to exhibit a well-rounded limb or delicately turned ankle, or show "wonderful agility." But there is always the fear of being chilled to death.

Indeed, ice is one of the greatest of summer luxuries. Ice may be taken from the clear ponds or still places in running streams and cut with half an old cross-cut saw.

Select a still day, as close to zero as may be. Have the menfolk cut the ice in large blocks of equal size, then take to the ice house and pack as closely as possible in layers, leaving about a foot space between the outside and the wall, filling the crevices between the blocks with sawdust. The sawdust should be packed closely between the mass of ice and the wall. When all is stored, it should be covered with a foot of sawdust.

Ice exposed to air will melt rapidly. A building correctly built need not cost more than twenty-five dollars.

The Kitchen

Furnish the Kitchen Well

Your husband may admire your grace and ease in society, or with your school-day accomplishments of music and painting, but all in perfection will not atone for an ill-ordered kitchen, sour bread, muddy coffee, tough meats, unpalatable vegetables, indigestible pastry, and the whole train of horrors that result from bad house-keeping. Study and contrive to bring order out of the natural chaos of the kitchen, and the head will save the hands and feet much work. Love lightens labor.

In no other room of the house are sun-light and fresh, pure air so indispensable. A long, narrow, dark kitchen is an abomination. Always furnish the kitchen well first, and if there is anything left to spend on the parlour, well; if not, the money has been spent wisely.

When working in the kitchen, wear a washable gown short enough to clear the floor by at least two inches. Always wear a cap or kerchief. Wash your hands. Scrub the nails with a brush then wooden toothpick. If you must touch your hair or pocket handkerchief, don't wipe your hands on your apron, wash your hands again. Be certain there is no tasting with the same spoon and no wasting.

Each morning clean the kitchen range by removing all cinders and ashes. Brush inside of fire box and flues, and brush out-side with wings or hair-brush. Sprinkle salt all over to remove dirt. If it adheres, remove

with sandpaper. Blacken and polish. No single piece of furniture contributes so much to the comfort of the family as the range, and it heats the bath water too.

A range with six lids and a large oven is the joy of a house-wife's heart. But, if your stove smokes, find out the reason and stop it. We get old and ugly soon enough; don't allow yourself to be smoked.

Any man who amounts to anything will not torment his wife by giving her green, wet wood. When you see a six-week-supply woodpile of finely split, dry wood, you know the husband appreciates his wife. You have to be a saint to keep your temper over an undecided fire that gives off blue smoke and sings psalms and sheds tears.

If your man is a lazy, good-for-nothing and fails to get the next year's burning and chopping wood ready, see how he would like to wash the dishes. That may get him chopping fast so it isn't left to the lady.

A large dresser to accommodate all appliances used in cookery is a necessity. The pantry should have an abundance of drawers and closets. Be certain the dishes are put away, as a house-keeper becomes sick at heart over a nick or break of a cup or saucer. There are very few families rich enough to bear it.

The best way to whiten an unpainted floor is to sprinkle the floor

freely with clean white sand. Thus the family, in the process of walking to and fro, keep the floor boards scoured to a snowy white-ness. Let it remain for a few days. Tables and shelves, like the floors, when in white wood are a delight to the eye.

Never paint nor paper the walls, but once a year apply a coat of good white-wash. White Wash: Eight pounds of whiting, one-fourth pound white glue. Cover the glue with cold water over-night and heat gradually until dissolved. Mix whiting with hot water. Add the glue and stir together till thick as cream.

Use Only the Purest Water

Pure water is as necessary to health as pure air. Rain water, filtered to remove any foreign matter caught from the roof or in the smokey atmosphere, is the purest attainable. Water that is at all doubtful, should be boiled before drinking. Wells, are very doubtful sources from which to procure a supply of pure water. When it is remembered that all water in wells must first come from the surface, and that it dissolves all sorts of filth as it passes into the earth, it will be readily understood that wells are apt to furnish impure water. People who throw dirty waste or other slops near a well, poison the water as surely as if they scattered arsenic.

Do not place arbolic powder boxes where your drain openings exist, merely to distract your nose's attention from the sewer gas issuing nature's warning, that like the premonitory smoke and rumblings of a volcano, advises you of the eruption of the disease to come.

Sand to Scour the Pots

There are now muffin pans of tin, Russian iron and granite ware. Their different shapes add a variety for the eye. The muffin rings of former years have done their duty and should be allowed to rest.

Wash oil-cloth tablecloth everyday in milk and water. Rub linseed oil on it every few weeks and polish with an old silk cloth.

A table cover, to be thrown over the table after it is set, is best made of calico. Pink mosquito netting is handsomer, but does not keep off dust.

To make a dish-cloth, unravel coarse manila rope and use the loose mass as a dish-cloth. Or, save cloth flour sacks, sugar, salt and corn-meal bags, and use them as dish-cloths, dusters, etc. Or use scrim or cotton under-wear crocheted about the edge, or folded and hemmed double. They should be numbered as this shows at once the number to be accounted for, and also makes it easy to use them in rotation, so that they may be worn equally. There should be at least six. Use two for the best dishes, two for greasy and two for pots and kettles. To wash the dishes, use three dish-cloths. A lady once said, "I have smelt a whole houseful of typhoid fever in one sour, dirty dish-rag." Add lemon juice and salt to the dish-water or a teaspoonful of kerosene.

Approximately one-fifth of the waking moments of thousands of intelligent women are spent washing dishes. These intelligent house-wives commence with the dish-washing as soon as the meal is finished.

Always scrape the dishes first or the water will become foul. Then scatter a little lye over the greasy dishes. Many good house-keepers do not allow soap to be used in washing dishes. Sand will scour the pots.

When "puss" is not on duty and your heart goes faint at the sight of another kitchen pest, put a barrel with a little meal in it in a corner, feed it to the pests in this manner long enough to relieve the "oldest and most experienced rat" of his suspicions, then fill the barrel half full of water with a little meal floating on top. The pests will then jump in and drown. More than a dozen can be caught in one night as the first rat that is trapped makes an outcry and the rest come to see what the matter is and share the same fate.

Potatoes in the Cellar

There is an old and true saying that, "A woman can throw out with a spoon faster than a man can throw in with a shovel." Be careful not to throw out the water used in cooking meats, as when it is cool, the fat can be saved as grease and is useful in many ways. Bits of meat make good hashed meat.

Vegetables must not be thrown away that would warm for breakfast nicely. Cold puddings that seem good for nothing, could be steamed for the next day. Dish-towels must not be thrown down where the mice can destroy them, nor chamberpails allowed to rust. Neglected potatoes in the cellar grow, and if the sprouts are not removed, the potatoes are

worthless. Bones can be burnt to make soap. Don't use china to feed cats and dogs. Economy counts no-where so well as in the kitchen.

Never throw away even a crumb of bread. Save it and put with other pieces. If you have a loaf about to mold, cut it in thin slices, place all together in a dripping-pan and set in oven to dry. You will find that when pounded and rolled it will be very nice for dressing, stuffing, puddings, griddle-cakes, and so on. Remember, though, for puddings, use only stale bread crumbs, rejecting crusts and not oven-dried, or you will have a pudding as tough as a door-mat.

Mother's Hash Doesn't Taste of Soap Grease

Yankees do everything in a hurry. They are not satisfied with praying fast, walking fast, working fast, traveling fast, but unconsciously eat fast too.

When you eat, masticate well—five minutes more at dinner may give you better use of an hour afterward.

See that the family thoroughly lubricates food with saliva necessary to promote good digestion. Omit all drinking until after eating.

It requires good food to make good muscle and good brain. The person who always sits down to badly cooked or scanty dinners, fights battle and life at a great disadvantage.

Mother's hash doesn't taste of soap grease, rancid butter, spoiled cheese, raw flour, boarding-house skillets, hotel coffee, or garden garlics. It is seasoned so delicately, and heated so quickly, that the only trouble is, there isn't ever enough to go round.

No measure of seasonings can be given, as a good cook must be a skillful taster. There must be a flavor of salt and a warm tone from pepper—in short, the spicing should be delicate rather than profuse. Those who like rank flavors may add spices to suit their coarse and uneducated palates.

For a steady jog over the course of life, good bread, butter, coffee, and potatoes and beef and mutton put strength in the limbs and nobility in the heart.

Boiled potatoes, to be at their best, should be served immediately when done. But if the men folk are late to dinner, take them up the moment they are done, wrap closely in a towel or cloth and lay them in the heater or in some warm place, and they will suffer only a little damage. Save the water in which beans have boiled to clean brass articles quickly and easily, especially small articles such as candle sticks and lamp burners. Put these items in a kettle completely immersed with bean water, cover and boil ten minutes. Rinse in hot water and rub dry with a soft cloth.

Do not have beef steak for dinner on washing or ironing days. Arrange to have something roasted in the oven, or else have cold meat. Do not have fried or boiled fish. The smells stick, and the clothes will not be sweet; besides the broiler and frying-pan take longer to clean. As for the vegetables, do not have spinach, pease, string-beans or apple-sauce. All these things take time to prepare and can be avoided as well as not.

The last chore for the day is to empty the tea-kettle and wipe it dry. This prevents rust as it is in constant demand during the day.

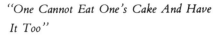

Bakery

Good Bread

To make good bread, always be up in the morning early, just "at the peep of the day."

Let all things be done decently and in order. The first to put in order is yourself; this is important in all cookery, but doubly important in bread-making. Be sure the hair is neatly combed and put up (which ought to be done before the dress is put on every morning). Secure hair net to prevent any hair from falling, and brush shoulders and back to be certain none are lodged there that might fall off. Wear a neat calico apron with bib and sleeves of dress well tucked up so they won't fall down. This adds much to the comfort of the most important task of the kitchen queen.

Three things are important: good flour, good yeast and good care. "Bread is the staff of life."

Potato Bread

Cook potatoes enough to make one cup when mashed. Use the water the potatoes were boiled in, and add enough luke-warm water to make three pints. Add one table-spoonful of salt and one table-spoonful of sugar, one-half cup of liquid yeast, and thicken quite stiff with flour. Let rise all night in a warm place. While bread is rising, don't cover with

old coats or shawls, make a small quilt to perform the duty. Commence early the next morning, and add flour enough to make stiff. Again let rise in a warm place until light. Knead into loaves, using some lard on the molding board but no flour. Knead with the palm until dough is a flat cake, then fold. Do not stop until you have fully finished, for bread that has "rested" is not good.

The little fairy that hovers over successful bread-making is heat, not too little nor too much, but uniform. To test heat there are two methods: 1. Place a tea-spoonful of flour on an old piece of crockery and set in middle of oven; if it browns in one minute, the heat is right. 2. An oven in which the bare arm can be held longer than to the count of twenty is not hot enough. If oven is too hot, sprinkle a quarter of an inch of sand on the bottom.

All systematic house-keepers shall hail the day when some enterprising Yankee or Buckeye girl shall invent a stove with a thermometer attached so that the heat may be regulated accurately and intelligently.

To make toast, take bread that is not too fresh. Trim off crust for crumb-jar. First warm each side of the bread, then move over a brisk fire, to have all parts toasted alike. If the slightest point is charred, scrape it off.

"O, weary mothers mixing dough,
Don't you wish that food would grow?
Your lips would smile I know to see
A cookie bush or a pancake tree."

Cookies

(Makes about a bushel)
One and one-fourth pounds of butter
One tea-spoonful cream of tartar
One-half tea-spoonful, scant soda
   in a fourth cupful milk

Two scant tea-spoonfuls mace
Six eggs
One nutmeg
Two pounds sugar
Flour, sufficient to roll

Bake until pronounced done!

Hotel Ginger-Snaps

(Ginger-Snaps will not be crisp if made on a rainy day)
One gallon of molasses
Two pounds brown sugar
One quarter melted butter
One cup soda

Half cup each:
   ground cloves, mace,
   ginger and cinnamon

Bake in tolerably quick oven.

Sponge Gingerbread

Take a piece of butter of the size of a hen's egg. Melt and mix with a pint of good molasses, a quart of flour, and a spoonful of ginger. Dissolve a heaping spoonful of salertus in a tumbler of milk. Strain and mix with other ingredients, adding sufficient flour to roll out easily. Bake on flat tins in a quick oven, after rolling it out about one-half inch thick. Leave on plate until further action.

Hard Gingerbread

This is nice to have in the family as it keeps so well.

One pound of flour,
Half a pound of butter with half a pound of sugar rubbed into.
Grate a spoon-ful or more of ginger,
A spoon-ful of rose water,
A hand-ful of caraway seeds,

Beat up well and knead until stiff. Bake on flat pans twenty or thirty minutes.

Pie Crust

Allow one hand as full of flour as it can take up for each pie. For each three hand-fuls, allow two heaping spoons-ful of lard or butter and some salt. Rub and stir with cold water. Roll out.

Cream Pie

Line a pie-plate with pie-paste

Add a layer of butter	Add a layer of flour
Add a layer of sugar	Add a layer of sugar

Pour some milk over and bake.

Before commencing to bake a cake, clean out the stove, take off the lids and brush inside. Rake it out underneath, get all the ashes out of the corners, have the best of fuel at hand. Have ready on a table, a broom splint picked off a new broom or a knitting needle to be used for testing cakes.

The finest ingredient for any cake is lots of common sense, and you cannot buy that at any time.

Hickory Nut Cake

Two cupfuls sugar	Three of flour
One of milk	Three eggs
Two-thirds of butter	Two tea-spoonsful baking-powder
One cupful nut-kernels, cut fine	

Tried and not found wanting!

President Hayes Cake

One cupful sugar
One-half of butter
Three eggs, beaten

Level tea-spoonful soda, stirred in
one-half cupful sour milk
Two small cupfuls flour

Flavor with lemon, pour in small dripping pan and bake one-half hour. Cut into squares. This cake is always elected for a "second term."

Tipsy Cake

One pound sugar, one pound flour, ten eggs (one at a time). Butter a high mold, well; dust mold with pulverized sugar. Bake and turn out of pan. Pour one quart sherry wine over cake, let stand to soak in. Stick sliced almonds all over the cake. Unsurpassed!

Kiss Cake

One armful of pretty girls
1 lovely face
2 laughing eyes

2 rosy cheeks
2 lips like strawberries

Mix well together and press 2 lips. The results will be astonishing.

Frosting

One piece of dark piazza and a little moon light and press into one large or small hand so as not to attract attention. 2 ounces of romance and one or two whiskers. Dissolve one-half a dozen glances into a quantity of hesitation and two ounces of yielding. Place kisses on blushing lips or cheeks. Flavor with a slight scream and set aside to cool.

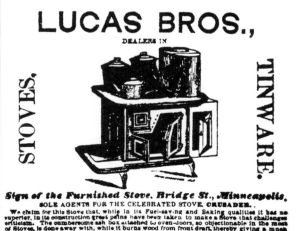

Some cooks scatter evil in their cooking such as by putting wine and brandy in cakes, pie and puddings which are calculated to make men drunkards. "Choose ye that which is good, that ye and your seed may live."

Love Cake

One pound of love,
2 lips well pressed,
4 hands clasped,

1 shady tree,
1 narrow bench,

Stir good and serve after dark.

Wedding Cake

Fifty eggs
Five pounds sugar
Five of flour
Five of butter
Fourth ounce cloves
Ounce of cinnamon

Four of mace
Four of nutmeg
Fifteen of raisins
Three of citron
Ten of currants
Pint of brandy

This makes forty-three and one-half pounds and keeps twenty years. This cake is unequaled.

Water Icing

Take any quantity of powdered sugar you require, add cold water enough to form a thick paste, beat. To every pound of sugar, add as much cream of tartar as will lie on a twenty-five cent piece. Spread evenly on cake.

Chocolate Icing

Ask any confectioner for a piece of "Baker's Eagle Cocoa" and if you cannot procure that, ask any grocer for pure cocoa in block. Place what you need of it in a basin of boiling water until the cocoa is dissolved. Add powdered sugar to taste and beat it well in; add whites of two eggs (whisked up a little) to every pound of cocoa used, beat it well. When you spread, be quick!

🍃 🍃 🍃 🍃

You may ornament your cake with icing sugar or sweet jelly. Ornamenting will require but little study by those having a taste for artistic work, which most ladies have. On the same principle as when you first perfected yourself in the scales for music before attempting the playing of a piece, you will succeed beyond your expectations. For harmlessly coloured cakes use light colours, as heavy colours are objectionable and in bad taste. Use "cochineal" (which is a red dye which comes from the dried bodies of certain female insects) for a light shade of pink. "Saffron" for yellow, and a drip of "indigo" will make blue, which added to the pink will give a mauve coloring with which you will be pleased.

Cookery

Seldom Is a Well-fed Man a Drunkard

The way to a man's heart is through his stomach, but a dirty kitchen and bad cooking have driven many a husband and son (and many a daughter too) from a home that should have been a refuge from temptation. Bad dinners go hand in hand with total depravity, while a properly fed man is already half saved. Keep the home fires burning, keep tending them while the family is cozy in the kitchen evenings, sing songs, play games.

A neat, clean home, a tidy table and well-cooked palatable meals, are safe-guards against the evils of the ale-house, liquor saloon, and the gambling-table. With our frying-pans and soup kettles, we wage a mighty war against intemperance, for seldom is a well-fed man a drunkard; and thus our attempts at palatable and economical cooking may "kill two birds with one stone." These words should be thoroughly digested before clogging them with others.

It Takes a Long Purse to Buy Fresh Products

Every good house-keeper will supply her table with a variety of vegetables all the year round for food suitable for a man who follows the plough, or bends over the anvil. The railroads and steamers connect the

climes so closely that one hardly knows whether he is eating fruits and vegetables in or out of season. The provider, however, realizes that it takes a long purse to buy fresh products at the North while the ground is yet frozen. It is late in the spring, when the old vegetables begin to shrink and grow rank, that we appreciate what comes from the South.

You must rely on the Lord and in the butcher. It is the butcher's interest to sell you his bad beef first. It's a good idea to change butchers once a month. The nearer the center of a city, the better the meat. Bad mutton is sold toward the limits of the city. Given a meal of gilt-edged broiled mutton, your husband will think this is quite a good world to get along in.

Be a good judge of chicken. If the butcher does not twist the wing before you, do it yourself.

Pork is unfit for female food, never trust your stomach with its digestion.

Many think the market not a pleasant or proper place for ladies. The idea is erroneous. There are as many gentlemen among market men as are to be found engaged in any other business. One should have a regular place at which to trade, especially if not a judge of meat. If the dealer is so informed, you can rely upon him to do well by you, and he will give you a nicer piece than you would have chosen.

Some Prices per Pound at the Market This Season:

Top of the round	$ .20	Fish - Average	.18
Rump	.25	A Pair of Ducks	1.50
Porter-house	.30	1 Single Calves Liver	.50
Sirloin	.25	1 Single Heart	.15
Tenderloin	.50	5 Pounds Salt	.40
Mutton Chops	.12	1 Pair Spectacles	.65
Mutton Leg	.17	1 Genuine Whalebone Corset	.39
Ham	.11	1 Beaver Fur	
Chocolate Candy	.20	Reversible Shawl	1.39
Gum Drops	.15	1 Fine Alligator and	
1 Gallon Apples	.27	Silk Pocketbook	.39

Mostly supply regulates price.

The Cost of Good Cooking

If the grocer be honest he buys honestly. His best butter will have little or no grease in it. First class butter is grass-sweet. If not, your grocer is a rascal. Let him know you resent grease in your butter and he will save you from that trial. Never hesitate in paying the highest price, even 28 cents, if you have to.

Have the grocer grind the coffee before your eyes. Buy only one pound at a time and keep it in a tin canister. Go to the tinner's and have him make a common, large coffee-pot which ought to cost no more than 35 cents. Good coffee is a love-philter of the strongest nature, it will make your husband love you, and he will famish when he goes elsewhere for a meal. Coffee beans mixed with eggs (shells too) make the coffee clear.

To test eggs, put the large end of the egg to your tongue; if it feels warm it is new.

If you don't have the time to get to town for shopping, the peddler comes on horseback ever so often with goods in his saddle bags: tinware, wash-boards, clothes-pins, flat-irons, shoes, and so on. Be patient, he'll come.

The dainty house-keeper who must buy her melons after a week or two of shipping, reshipping, transporting and handling, until it has cost nearly its weight in gold, should heed these instructions: Get your melon as fresh as possible, let it remain on ice several hours. If the meat of the melon appears wilted or withered, or is not perfectly ripe, pass it to the four-footed beasts where it should have gone in the first place.

Morning is the best time to eat fruit, and fresh fruit is then in the best condition to be eaten. Berries will be very nice with only sugar, or perhaps a little cream. There is a vast difference, however, between fruit with cream and fruit with milk. Cream is easily digested and slow to sour, while the contrary is true of milk. People have been known to live after eating strawberries and buttermilk, and have also been known to die after eating hot apple dumplings and cold milk. If you happen to be the fortunate possessor of a berry patch, let the children go out and pick and eat before they have their breakfast porridge. Properly trained children will not abuse this privilege.

Begin the Meal with Soup

Much of the slop served as soup a la this, that and the other, would not, except for the name, be recognized as something to be put in the stomach. A man may eat his fill and yet be hungry. It is not the quantity but the proper quality in food that satisfies.

Physiologically it is necessary to begin a meal with soup as it gives rest to a fainting stomach before the beef or mutton is attacked, and the stomach is shocked with an ill-masticated half-pound weight of beef.

Never use rice, barley or noodles in the same soup.

If your husband seems to have gone "mad," make a broth of hedge-hog, make him eat both broth and flesh. If that doesn't bring him to his senses nothing will.

Orange Marmalade

9 oranges	8 pounds of sugar
6 lemons	16 cups water

Slice fruit very thin, cover with water and let stand overnight. Boil slowly for two hours then add sugar and boil one hour longer. When cool, pour in jelly glasses or jars and let stand a few days. A delicious sweetmeat for breakfast.

Buckwheat Cakes

Take two quarts of water, blood warm, half pint brewer's yeast, make a thin batter, let rise as far as they will come, add three fourths of a teaspoonful of soda dissolved in a little water, then fry as quick as you like.

The diet of the aged should suit their condition. If delicate, give lean mutton broth. If fat, heavy and inclined to slumber, give fish, nuts, vegetables and fruits. If lean, irritable, querulous or sleepless, let them eat of bread and butter, buckwheat cakes, milk and potatoes. It should improve their sleep and disposition.

No more sad times preparing Hubbard squash. You don't need to call on the ax to help. Wash and bake it first, then remove seeds and the sweet juices have been retained and so has the temper.

Oatmeal

Put two teacupsful of oatmeal and one tablespoonful of salt in a quart tin pail filled three fourths full of water. Cover close and set in a kettle one-third full of water and boil three hours. Stir after it commences to boil.

Oatmeal is good for growing children who need bone and muscle producing food. To be wholesome it must be well cooked, not the pasty, half-cooked mess usually served in boarding-houses. Be sure to cook it the full three hours. There are a few persons with very delicate digestive powers.

Saturday Bean Soup

Put the pot on with more beans than enough, add water, slice of salt pork, and parboil till beans are ready for oven. Take out pork and part of beans, leaving soup. Just add more water and some vegetables three-quarters of an hour before dinner. The beans, taken out, with brown bread, will form Sunday's breakfast.

Corn Mush

Put four quarts fresh water in a kettle to boil. Salt to suit the taste. Stir one and one-half quarts corn meal, letting it sift through the fingers slowly to prevent lumps, adding a little faster until as thick as can be stirred with one hand. Bake one hour in kettle or pan. Excellent for frying when cold. Use a hard-wood paddle, two feet long, with a blade two inches wide and seven inches long to stir with.

ℐ ℐ ℈ ℈

Figures never lie. When we consume meat and sugar in excessive quantities, anyone can readily tell the story. A one-sided diet never fails to bring evil results.

Baked Pig

Collar a nice little pig about six weeks old, scald in hot water to kill, score in squares, rub all over with lard, make a corn meal dressing. Stuff the pig until plump, sew it up, place it on its knees in a pan filled with water. Baste it with gravy and also two red pepper pods. Serve with an apple in its mouth, 2 cranberries for eyes. A wreath of parsley looks well around the neck.

Meats

To keep meat fresh for a week or two in summer, put into sour milk or buttermilk, then place in cool cellar. Rinse well when used.

Boiling is the way to make fresh meats rich and nutritious. "The pot should only smile, not laugh." The bubbles should appear in one part of the surface of the water only, not all over it. A pod of red pepper in the water will prevent the unpleasant odour of boiling from filling the house.

Roasting: The roast will need a washing if it comes from an uncleanly butcher. The joint is placed close to a brisk fire, turned so as to expose every part to the heat.

Frying: The fire must be hot enough to sear the surface. When improperly done, the result is an unwholesome, greasy mess.

ℐ ℐ ℈ ℈

For each pound of dry food we should have five pounds of water. People we see that look like a shadow, as a rule do not take water.

Nice Gravy

Gravy is a problem many house-keepers never solve. Remember that grease is not gravy; neither is raw flour. Almost any kind of meat liquor may be made into nice gravy by simply adding a little seasoning and some thickening. The gravy will require but little cooking, but when thickened with raw flour, it must be done or it will taste like gummy paste. Brown a quart at a time. All gravies should be well stirred over a hot fire; boiled not simmered. The care of fat and drippings is as necessary in any family as the care of last year's garden seeds or the "Family Record."

ℐ ℐ ℚ ℚ

Look frequently into the pails to see that nothing is thrown to the pigs that should be in the grease-pot. Look into the grease-pot, and see that there is nothing in there which might nourish your family or a poorer one.

Anchovy Sandwiches

4 anchovies	1 hard-boiled egg
4 ounces butter	salt and pepper
little nutmeg	

Bone anchovies and pound with butter, egg, salt and pepper and a little nutmeg. Spread on bread and roll up. Then decide whether to eat it or to throw it out the window.

ℐ ℐ ℚ ℚ

Pickles are not famous for wholesome qualities, even when made with the greatest care. If they must be eaten, it is best to make them at home, as those sold in the market are often coloured a beautiful green with sulphate of copper, which is a deadly poison, or are cooked in brass or copper vessels, which produces the same result in an indirect way.

Cucumber Pickles

Cover the bottom of cask with common salt. Gather the cucumbers every other day, early in the morning or late in the evening, as it does not injure the vines so much then as in the heat of the day, lay them carefully so as not to bruise, rub off the little black briers, that is the secret of keeping them perfectly sound. Lay them in a cask three or four inches deep, cover with salt, repeat. Spread a cloth over them, then a board with a stone on it. When a new supply of cucumbers is to be added, remove the stone, board and cloth, wash them until every particle of scum is off, throw away the soft ones. Put in fresh cucumbers, layer by layer, with salt to cover each layer.

Winter Salad

Two large potatoes, passed through kitchen sieve,
Unwonted softness to the salad give;
Of mordant mustard add a single spoon—
Distrust the condiment which bites too soon;
But deem it not, though made of herbs, a fault
To add a double quantity of salt;
Three times the spoon with oil of Lucca crown,
And once with vinegar procured from town,
True flavor needs it, and your poet begs
The pounded yellow of two well-boiled eggs,
Let onion atoms lurk within the bowl,
And, half-suspected, animate the whole;
And lastly, on the favored compound toss
A magic tea-spoon of anchovy sauce,
Then, though green turtle fail, though venison's tough
Though ham and turkey are not boiled enough,
Serenely full, the epicure shall say,
"Fate can not harm me, I have dined to-day."

Chow Chow Pickles

Let two hundred small cucumbers stand in salt and water closely covered for three days. Boil for fifteen minutes in half a gallon of the best cider vinegar, one ounce of white mustard seeds (tying each ounce separately in Swiss bags), one handful small green peppers, two pounds of sugar, a few onions, a piece of alum half the size of a nutmeg, then pour the vinegar while hot over the cucumbers, let stand a day, repeating the operation three or four mornings. Mix one-fourth pound mustard with the vinegar, pour over cucumbers, and seal up the bottles. Pickles will be perfect for three years.

Capers

To pickle Nasturtium-buds to be eaten as capers, gather your little knobs quickly after your blossoms are off; put in cold water and salt for three days, shifting once a day; then make a pickle of some white-wine, some white-wine vinegar, eschalot, horse-radish, pepper, salt, cloves and whole mace and nutmeg quartered; then put in your seeds and stop them close.

Grandma's White Pudding

This was considered an "extra dish" at all the quilting frolics and log rollings of the 1700s.

Weigh equal quantities of the best beef suet and sifted flour. Shave down suet and rub into fine particles with hands, removing all tough and stringy parts. Mix with flour. Season highly with pepper. Salt to taste. Stuff loosely in beef-skins (entrails cleansed) half a yard or less in length. Secure the ends. Prick every two or three inches with a darning needle.

Place to boil in a kettle of cold water hung on the crane. Boil three hours. Place on table till cold, then hang in a cool place, tied up in a bag with a clean bottom. Put away where it will be dry and cool. When wanted, cut off quantity needed, boil, place before the fire to dry off and "crisp."

Bread Pudding

An economical one, when eggs are dear. Cut some bread and butter very thin. Place in pie-dish till three parts full. Break into a basin one egg. Add two teaspoonsful of flour, three of brown sugar. Mix well. Add by degrees a pint of milk and a little salt. Pour over bread. Bake about half an hour. A nice sized pudding for two hungry or four polite persons.

Boiled Custard Pudding

Boil a pint of new milk with a little lemon-peel and a few laurel leaves. Pour it boiling hot upon five eggs, well-beaten. Sweeten it to taste. When nearly cold, add a dessertspoonful of French brandy. Butter a basin or mould, and boil for half an hour.

An ice cream freezer is a great luxury in the family and will soon do away with that most unhealthy dish, pie.

Common Beer

Allow at the rate of two gallons of water to a handful of hops, a little fresh spruce, or sweet fern and a quart of bran. Boil it two or three

hours. Strain it through a sieve. Stir in, while hot, a teacup of molasses to each gallon of liquor. Let it stand till lukewarm. Turn it into a clean barrel. Add a pint of good yeast and shake well together. This may be used the very next day. If needed sooner make Quick Ginger Beer.

Quick Ginger Beer

To a pail of water, add two ounces of ginger, one pint of molasses, a gill of good yeast. Fit for use in two hours.

One Week's Menu

Breakfast—buttered toast, pork chops—broiled, hominy grits.
Dinner—tomato soup, pigeon pie, creamed potatoes, pickles, corn, steamed pudding with sauce, almonds, raisins.
Supper—plain bread, sardines with lemon, light coffee cake or sweet buns and jam.

Breakfast—flannel cakes, mutton chops—broiled, potatoes.
Dinner—beefsteak, soup, broiled steak, whole boiled potatoes, salsify. oyster salad, sweet pickles, transparent pudding, cream puffs, oranges.
Supper—beat biscuit, cold meat, apple fritters with sugar, sponge cake.

Breakfast—fried frogs, fried potatoes, corn gems, boiled eggs.
Dinner—baked pig, mashed potatoes, dressing, parsnips—fried, lettuce, lemon pudding.
Supper—sardines, pop-overs, baked rhubarb.

Breakfast—broiled porter-house steak, hominy croquette, long breakfast rolls.
Dinner—chicken soup, chicken dressed with egg sauce, whole potatoes, spinach, young lettuce and onions, sweet pickles and orange float.
Supper—cold chicken and currant jelly, cold rolls, snow custard, cake.

Breakfast—corn muffins, oysters in shell, croquettes of turkey, potato rissoles.
Dinner—turkey soup, quail on toast, walled oysters, boiled onions, celery and slaw, ice cream and cake.
Supper—graham mush, milk and jam.

Breakfast—buckwheat cakes, broiled spare ribs or sausage, pates of turkey hot with gravy, hominy.
Dinner—escalloped turkey, fried raw potatoes, beans, mince pie, cakes.
Supper—tea buns, cold venison, fruit, lady fingers.

Breakfast—cold heart, dropped eggs, Sally Lunn, tomato omelet, hot rusk-marmalade.
Dinner—stewed kidney, corn pone, cabbage hash, Indian Pudding.
Supper—macaroni soup, turnips, fried apples, tid-bit of cheese, dried figs and nuts, floating island.

After dinner sit awhile, after supper walk a mile.

In the Garden

Gather Herbs before a Full Moon

Your garden can be likened to Eden, with fresh living greens and hollyhocks swaying along the fence, morning glories winding their way up the porch and nasturtiums overflowing the flower boxes. One must have fresh crisp lettuce, great ripe tomatoes and long silken tassels of corn that wave and rustle with every passing breeze. Scarlet geraniums, brilliant poppies, and yellow mums which nod and wink in the sunlight. Then there are the buttercups, shooting stars and many sweet, shy flowers with unknown names. The wild mint smells so fresh, and sweeter than can be told. It is difficult for one not to linger by the pansies. The flowers' glories are not dimmed because they open by the side of the homely cabbage or humble cucumbers, all are equally tended and loved.

As the rose is composed of the sweetest flowers and the sharpest thorns; as the heavens are sometimes overcast, alternately tempestuous and serene: so is the life of men intermingled with hopes and fears, with joys and sorrows, with pleasure and pain.

Thyme, marjoram, sweet-basil, summer savory, sage, caraway, coriander, dill, fennel, rosemary, lavender—these sweet names suggest good cheer, pleasant gardens, fragrant linen, calm wrinkled faces in quaint bonnets looking lovely holding a fragrant leaf in work-worn hands. Think of ALL those hands have done!

Take time to roam the garden at your own sweet will. Among the lovely flowers and odorous shrubs we see the colour of the rose ladened with the morning dew, and the fruits which satisfy our hunger, right from God's own hand. Repose when weary on soft couches of moss, and be lulled to slumber by the soft rustle of the leaves above our heads and the sweet songs of the birds.

Berries of any kind are nice to grow in the garden. They must always be picked when they are fresh with morning dew. Strawberries are a joy, with or without wine. The leaves make a nice tea that is cheap nourishment. It is remarkable how earth offers to man this fruit in abundance from our loving Creator.

If the weather be dry, perhaps on your way home from the fields, or when going out to look at your standing crop, take a ramble to gather medicinal herbs, growing on dry ground or a sunny hill-side. When herbs are gathered in their best blossom, a tea can be made to end all your sufferings. It is best to gather herbs before a full moon.

Nearly every sort of green stuff which grows in a garden has some medicinal value, and any of them keeps the blood cool and the bowels active. To protect against sunstroke, for example, a wet napkin could be placed on the top of the head under the hat; just as effective are wet cabbage leaves.

Every Mother Knows How to Make a Nice Little Tea

A cup of tea is a panacea for most of the ills to which women are liable whether we are tired, faint or depressed. The average woman, constantly distracted by children, animals or servants are at times overcome by grief or headache, and can turn to the friendly aid of her cup of tea. There is nothing more delightful than the five o'clock tea.

Every mother knows how to make a nice little tea. For one cup she takes as much of the dried herbs as she can hold with three fingers, pours half a pint of boiling water on them, covers, and, in just fifteen minutes, the tea is ready.

Primrose and cowslip blossoms dried in the sun and mixed with tea are nice. Even the little violets—pretty fragrant spring flowers—are helpful if the anxious mother boils a handful of green or dried violet leaves or their roots, in a half a pint of water and gives two or three spoonfuls of this little tea every two hours, a cough—even whooping cough—will be relieved. Also, a violet leaf on a piece of linen bound across the forehead and the back of head brings relief to a headache. Rejoice at the fragrance and lovely blue colour of the violet, but also keep a supply when sickness comes your way.

It is also necessary to grow the known cures for cold, sore-throat

"Patience Is A Flower That Grows Not In Everyone's Garden"

and the like, such as onions, garlic and cabbage (for sauerkraut) in the making of poultices.

Catnip should be gathered before dog-days and when in bloom. Dry in the shade, and place in a paper sack. Sweetened catnip tea taken every night will end troublesome colic.

Camomile tea used in cases of fever, gripes, cramps, colds, etc., is so well-known and liked that it is quite unnecessary to say anything further about it.

Of the garden herbs, basil tea is said to make one more alert, sage and marjoram teas calm one down, and mint tea is said to arouse passions.

Add Herbs to the Bathing Water

Many an over-taxed woman whose skin becomes grey and wilted, adds herbs to the bathing water. One table-spoonful of the following,

or as many as can be had of: rosemary, peppermint, chamomile, sage, pine needles, lavender, thyme, dandelion, and marigold and don't forget the daisy petals. You will be refreshed and feel years younger.

Perfume-bearing flowers are much more fragrant when moistened with dew. Perfumes and colognes can readily be made from the essences from the garden as can smelling salts.

Pot Pourri

Half a pound of bay-salt;
A quarter of a pound of saltpetre bruised with a little common salt.
Add it to threepennyworth of cloves pounded;
The same of storax, one small nutmeg grated;
Two or three bay-leaves braken;
Lavender flowers freshly gathered, rose leaves gathered dry.

Rose, pansie and many other flower petals may be used in making pot pourri and sachets: Add some basil, rosemary, marjoram, cloves, cinnamon, nutmeg, mint, and sage. Their fragrance makes you feel beautiful in mind and body.

❦ ❦ ❦ ❦

Sage tea or a hand-ful of rosemary leaves in a pint of hot water makes a nice little shampoo.

❦ ❦ ❦ ❦

The lovely little marigold petals, either fresh or dried, may be eaten, although not more than one ounce per day is recommended. They may be used in salads, omelettes or where-ever a little colouring or their special flavor is needed. The chopped leaves give a zest to a salad. Daisies and dandelions intimately entwined make a delightful salad. White bread sand-wiches holding tender young nasturtium leaves between their buttered folds go well with salads or meat or fish. Garnish the plate with nasturtium leaves and blossoms.

A Good Shot-Gun and a Keen Eye on the "Patch"

Those who raise their own melons will need no instruction on the subject of serving and eating them. After the fruit is well grown, a good shot-gun and a keen eye on the "patch" is all that is necessary to secure a ripe crop.

Preserve the white potatoes by storing in a cool place. Sweet potatoes pack in dry forest leaves, celery in sand, apples in sawdust and lemon in water which is changed weekly.

At last when autumn draws near and you have row upon row of canned goods ready in abundance for the coming year, the hammock is so temptingly inviting that one has a blessed sense of relief to remember it too must be made useful.

Keeping A Keen Eye On The Patch.

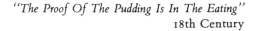

The Dining-Room

Never Starch the Napkins

In every house, great or small, the dining-room should be as bright, cheerful and cosey as possible. At the table the mistress should wear her brightest smile. If there are trials and trouble, do not bring them to the table. They impair digestion and send husband and children out to business or school, glum and gloomy, instead of refreshed and strengthened. Little attentions to the decoration or pretty arrangement of the table, charm the eye and whet the appetite, and the heart is immediately gladdened. The everyday observance of sensible and simple table manners ought always to be encouraged, because, in the long run, it promotes the comfort and the cultivation of the family.

Sit up straight. Do not bend your head to meet your fork. Never use a knife to carry food to the mouth. It is a serious breach of etiquette to examine a dish and then refuse it.

There should not be a woolen carpet in the dining-room. It will absorb odours and is more difficult to clean than a bare floor. Two or three breadths of fine Japanese matting, sewed together to make a square makes a satisfactory dining-room rug. A silence cloth under the linen makes the table-cloth look better and last longer.

When giving a party, invite only the congenial. Twelve seems to be a good number of guests. Invitations should be sent by messenger and

never mailed to persons in the same town. Out of town postage costs 2 cents per ounce. When sending a reply, a day's delay is the extreme limit. To arrive ten minutes early is quite enough, but ten minutes beyond the appointed time is the utmost limit of tardiness admissible in a guest.

A round table is suggested as conversation is easily made general. Either have a center-piece of ferns or flowers with delicate odours or fruit. However, it is suggested that the pretty custom of a little bouquet in a silver holder by the side of each lady's plate and three or four flowers found in the napkin of each gentleman give a tasteful arrangement. Never starch the napkins. See that the salt cellars are dry and free from lumps and the pepper boxes are in good order. Plates should be left on the top shelf of the range so they will be warm when needed.

Avoid cane seats in a dining-room, where fine fabrics and laces are kept on them so long a time. They play havoc. Under each chair should be placed a stool or hassock for the ladies, or for such as may require it.

On the arrival of the guests, the ladies and gentlemen should be shown to different rooms, where they may remove their "wraps." They are then shown to the parlour, where they are received by the host and hostess. Until dinner is announced this time is spent in introductions and social intercourse.

Each gentleman offers the lady assigned to him his right arm, and escorts her to a seat at his left, passing her in front of him to her chair which he has gracefully drawn back. The host leads the way to the dining-room and the hostess follows last, and all guests stand until she is seated. Ease and manner of the host and hostess should be quiet and never hurried. Any betrayal of anxiety or embarrassment or any blundering is a wet blanket to all enjoyment. A dozen blunders will not cause half as much discomfort as an agitated and uncomfortable mistress. Nothing short of an accident that threatens a guest with instant death ought to ruffle her calm demeanor.

Once seated at the table, the gloves are drawn off and laid in the lap under the napkin, which is spread lightly, not tucked in. Soup should be eaten from the side of the spoon without noise, or tipping of the plate. the mouth should not go to the food, but the food to the mouth. Eat without noise and with the lips closed. Friends will not care to see how you masticate your food, unless they are of a very investigative turn of mind. Eat slowly both for health and manners sake.

Too great a variety of dishes is coarse display. A few cooked to a nicety and served with grace, make the most charming dinners. The meal should begin with soup, then fish, followed by one vegetable, then a roast and a salad garnished with either wild roses, buttercups or nasturtiums—nice if not used too freely—cheese and then dessert. Bread and butter is a dish for dessert.

A Sumptuous Dinner
Would Follow This General Routine:

1. Shell fish, small clams or oysters, one-half dozen for each person, laid in their shells on a bed of finely crushed ice. With these are offered red and black pepper, grated horse-radish, small thin slices of buttered brown bread, or tiny crisp biscuits and quarters of lemon.
2. Soup.
3. A course of hors d'oeuvres, such as radishes, celery, olives and salted almonds.
4. Fish, with potatoes and cucumber, the latter dressed with oil and vinegar.
5. Mushrooms or sweetbreads.
6. Asparagus or artichokes.
7. Spring lamb, or roast, with a green vegetable.
8. Roman punch.
9. Game with salad.
10. A second entree.
11. A rich pudding.
12. A frozen sweet.
13. Fresh and crystallized fruit, and bonbons.
14. Coffee and liqueurs.

Many sensible hostesses who speak with authority maintain eight courses are enough for most dinners. These would consist of grapefruit or oysters, soup, fish, entree, roast, salad, dessert and coffee. White wine is drunk with the first course and sherry with the soup. Champagne is offered with fish, and its glasses are replenished throughout the meal. Claret or burgundy comes in with the game. The temperature of these liquids must never be below sixty degrees.

Make certain when serving spirits to a guest that he never sees the bottom of his drinking glass too often.

First the host should ask the blessing for the meal, then the eldest lady, or the lady at the right of the host, should be served first. Glasses should be filled with water just before they are seated. Never experiment on new dishes for guests.

It is ill-bred to help oneself too abundantly, or to flood food with gravies. Nothing creates such disgust as a plate bedaubed with gravy or scattered food. Never load up your fork with food until you are ready to convey it to your mouth, unless you are famishing and you think your life depends on your not losing a second.

Caress the Asparagus

There are a variety of ways to eat asparagus. Some say the tip should be cut off and eaten with a fork. But from an art point of view, there cannot be a more charming sight than to see a pretty woman "caressing" a piece of asparagus.

There is an old French saying that it is as disgraceful for a host not to know how to carve well as it is to have a fine library and not know how to read. If your host does not carve well, tell your man he should forgo the pleasure of inviting his friends to dinner, or serve chops or ribs which do not require carving. Better yet, teach him how to carve; it only requires knowledge and practice. Carving should be taught in the family, each child taking his turn. All hosts should be able to perform the task with sufficient skill at least to prevent remark. He should retain his seat, manage his hands and elbows artistically, and be perfectly at his ease.

If fowl is served, it is proper to ask, "What part do you prefer?" When asked that question, answer immediately, do not hesitate.

Water glasses are refilled at the right hand, everything else is served at the left.

The hostess should continue eating until all guests have finished.

Gentlemen Don't Pick Their Teeth

One who is healthy does not wish to dine at a dissecting table. Do not needlessly report ill of others. It is not the mission of every one to detail and report it all. There is evil enough in men, God knows.

Two hours is long enough to serve any dinner that Christians ought to eat. Three hours and a half is too long.

Before the dessert is served, all crumbs should be brushed from the cloth. Then the finger-bowls are brought in on plates with doilies, and are used by dipping the fingers in lightly and drying them on the napkin. The finger-bowls should be half full of warm water, with a bit of lemon floating in it, or rose water or lavender may be used.

No where is the distinction between a gentleman and boor more marked than at the table. See that none of the gentlemen pick their teeth at the table. "Pshaw!"

When all have finished dessert, the hostess gives the signal that the dinner is ended by pushing back her chair, and the ladies repair to the drawing-room, the eldest leading and the youngest following last. The gentlemen repair to the library or smoking-room. In about half an hour, tea is served in the drawing-room, with a cake-basket of crackers or little cakes; the gentlemen join the ladies, and after a little chat over their cups, all are at liberty to take leave.

Many a fine lady has blushed because of the loud complaints issuing from her after a meal due to the tight-lacing hampering the digestive system from its proper function.

When washing the dishes, arrange to have the silver washed where the noise cannot reach the guests.

Picnics and Other Frolicks

Be Up at Five O'Clock

In the "sunny south" open-air outings are in order as early as April, but in the more northern latitudes they should never be attempted before the latter part of May or June, and September and October are the crowning months for them around the northern lakes, where hunting and fishing give zest to the sports.

First, be up at five o'clock in the morning, in order to have chicken, biscuits, etc., freshly baked. Provide two baskets, one for the provisions, and the other for dishes and utensils, which should include, at least, the following:

table-cloth with oil-cloth to put under it
napkins
towels
plates
cups
forks
a few knives and table-spoons
tea-spoons
sauce dishes
tin cups (or tumblers, if the picnickers are of the over-fastidious
    variety);

a tin bucket for water, in which a bottle of cream, lemons, oranges, or other fruit may be carried to the scene of action;

another with an extra close cover, partly filled with made chocolate, which may be reheated by setting in an old tin pail or pan in which water is kept boiling a la custard-kettle

a frying pan

a coffeepot, with the amount of prepared coffee needed tied in a course, white flannel bag

a tea-pot, with tea in a neat paper package

tin boxes of salt, pepper, and sugar

a tin box for butter (if carried) placed next to a block of ice, which should be well wrapped with a blanket and put in a shady corner of the picnic wagon.

You must dress in a stout walking-costume of woolen material, with a hat large enough to shelter the eyes, and a cane or staff if there will be any climbing.

When over-taken with thirst, don't stop along the peaceful bubbling brook as frogs and worms are lurking there and it is too great a consequence for the stomach and you will take to your bed.

Too much of anything, however good, is too much. Here are some recipes for picnic ideas:

Broiled Prairie Chicken

Pluck, wash and dry and cut open down the back. Rub with salt, pepper and butter, broil over brisk coals. When cold, serve with currant jelly.

Sponge Cake

Fourteen eggs, their weight in sugar, weight of eight in butter, of six in flour, juice and rind of two lemons. Stir rapidly and bake quick.

Strawberry Acid

Dissolve four ounces citric acid in half gallon water, pour over two gallons ripe strawberries. Let stand 24 hours and drain liquor off. To every pint of juice add a pound and a half of loaf sugar. Boil, let stand three days and bottle. This will be ready for a refreshing drink when one table-spoonful of acid is added to a glass of ice water.

To a picnic everyone is expected to bring their very best spirits. A lady who strolls away for a couple of hours with a young man to the woods, should scarcely be asked to join a second picnic. There should always be a fair sprinkling of chaperons or elderly people to retain the carelessness and noisy romping of the younger ones. However, to enjoy the day to the fullest, be as silly and as wild as the youngest.

When Bathing by the Sea

Perhaps your picnic will be beside the sea where you will be able to take a sea bath. If you are a modest girl, your bathing suit should not attract attention to you. It should be of dark blue or black serge, high about the throat, sleeves reaching to your elbows, a loose bodice that will not cling when wet, a pair of knee breeches, a full skirt and a pair of stockings. You may pout at all this but it is wiser to bathe when no men, other than from your family, are about.

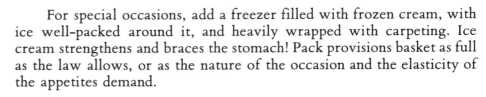

For special occasions, add a freezer filled with frozen cream, with ice well-packed around it, and heavily wrapped with carpeting. Ice cream strengthens and braces the stomach! Pack provisions basket as full as the law allows, or as the nature of the occasion and the elasticity of the appetites demand.

Archery is a sport women are very good at, but include the men folks in a game of croquet, or lawn-tennis.

A taffy pull is another enjoyment for both sexes.

Molasses Taffy

2 cups brown sugar
1 cup molasses

1 tablespoon vinegar
one-fourth cup water

Flavor to taste. Boil until it makes a crisp ball in cold water. Stir in one tea-spoonful soda. Pour on buttered plates to cool. Then, every-body PULL.

Eating lump sugar wet with cologne just before going to a party makes the eyes bright.

It does not always follow that every girl who is a parlour singer will be a success. Unless a girl who can sing well at home possesses unusual talent and voice of more than ordinary beauty she will do well to remain there. Nature must give a girl a voice or else she will never acquire one. One pure, natural note, is a joy forever; but a falsetto note is a ghost of departed sweetness and painful to the hearers. If you have been blessed with vocal powers never wear low-necked dresses and do not over-tax your powers.

Some ladies while singing, twist themselves into so many contortions, and writhe their bodies and faces into such actions, one would be inclined to believe they are suffering from a toothache or gout.

Duets on the harp and piano are very delightful. The guitar makes a graceful variety but it is monotonous and soon fatigues one's attention. The zitter is an instrument for the boudoir, it is soft and romantic. The violin is unsuitable to young ladies. Instrumental music is appropriate for any age, but after forty years the voice loses the delicious freshness of youth.

ℐ ℐ ℚ ℚ

Strange how on Thanksgiving, Christmas and various other holidays, families get together and abuse their stomachs. These practices injure the stomach, induce disease, abbreviate life and make wise men talk silly.

ℐ ℐ ℚ ℚ

If you do not know what to do with idle hands in the presence of others, carry you fan with you to keep them occupied.

ℐ ℐ ℚ ℚ

Do not forget your social graces at the country fairs or the basket socials, one must be pleasant even if the highest bidder for your basket is a stupid oaf.

ℐ ℐ ℚ ℚ

Pleasure, like all truly precious things in this world cannot be bought or sold. If you wish to be amused, you must do your part.

ℐ ℐ ℚ ℚ

Women of questionable character go out with bare shoulders. A woman who flirts is despicable.

A Lemon Squeeze

For lighter entertaining one might try a Lemon Squeeze: Invite all your friends, young and old, and tell each guest to bring a lemon. Each squeezes their own lemon and carefully saves the seeds. The lady with the most seeds and the gentlemen with the most seeds should each receive a prize. You may award the person with the least seeds a "booby prize." There will then be lemonade to drink and it would be nice to surprise the guests by serving lemon cakes, lemon pies, lemon ice cream or anything using lemons which your culinary skill is capable of producing. This is intended for a home frolic but may be extended to church entertainment by having each guest bring six lemons and then selling the lemonade. It may even squeeze money for charitable purposes out of tightly buttoned pockets.

If a Suitor Comes to Call

Cease all acquaintances with a suitor if he does not conduct himself as a gentleman. It is in good taste to have your mother remain in the room when you have visitors. It is not proper to receive a gift if you have only known the young man a short time; but if you've known him longer and he presents you with flowers—even a little nosegay, poetry, or sweets—verbal thanks are out of place. It is proper to write him a note at a later time thanking him. Cards are always left when visits are made. If the young man starts to leave, permit him to depart, the hostess should make no effort to detain him.

When Traveling

The art of packing for a railroad or steamboat journey is to pack your treasures so that there is a convenient place for everything, with small articles in the corners so that an article can be found without complete upheaval. One must have one's Bible, a button-hook, a glove buttoner, a nail-file, a toothbrush in a tin box, a stylographic pen, a pair of scissors with a ribbon bow for easy identification, a penknife and a lead pencil with rubber sheath packed in the corners. In the pockets, place three or four handkerchiefs, a second pair of gloves, an extra veil and a small envelope of court-plaster, citric acid for scurvey, Hartshorn for snake bites, and a little quinine, opium and whiskey. Another envelope should contain postals, one or two telegraph blanks, delicately perfumed stationery, a writing tablet and a blotter, and stamp-box with regular and special delivery stamps. In the middle, place a Mother Hubbard wrapper, for use as a night-robe, your unwhisperables, a small towel, a case containing ribbon, a sewing needle, spools of thread, safety pins, buttons, thimble, whisk brush, a black folding fan and a pair of rubber over-shoes wrapped in some dark cotton material. Don't leave your politeness and polish at home. Always travel with one large trunk rather than two small ones and you may need a hand-satchel besides.

Never Stay As Long As You Are Invited

It is difficult to be a visitor. One must always get up and dress as soon as the breakfast bell rings, and we never know people until we have lived in the same house with them. Of course we do not entirely know them even then but we never forget them after staying under the same roof.

The first day as a guest you are just that, the second day you become a burden, and the third, a pest. Never stay as long as you are invited. When visiting there comes a time to disappear and leave one's hostess to herself. Surely you have a bit of fancy-work, sketch-board or a book to which you can devote some time. To be left alone is the birth-right of every human being for certain hours of the day, to do as one wishes.

It is not an easy task to sleep in an unaccustomed bed, to alter your breakfast hour, to await the hostess's pleasure about the carriage, to talk to the stupid son or daughter. One may be afraid of the family brute they call "puppy," and it is hard to find something pleasant to say about the weather, especially in a prolonged drizzle. Do not stare around the room or ask the price of furniture. Quietly ignore little frictions between husband and wife, and never mentions defects in their friends or servants. If you are unable to so contain yourself, stay home!

Ailments and Cures

When people fall sick they seem to lose what little common sense they possessed when well. Men and women who are reasonably wise and reasonable in other matters, cherish the most absurd superstitions, and follow the advice of the most transparent quacks when it comes to disease and medicine. The house-hold medicine chest should contain only simple remedies, the effect of which, at worst, can not be very injurious.

Too often the doctor brings the medicine only to have the medicine bring the doctor again.

Make Friends with Fresh Air

Plenty of fresh air, a sane and simple diet and regular exercise, combined with a care-free state of mind, are the secrets of a normal healthy life. They are so simple that people over-look them.

Make friends with the fresh air. Some ignorant persons have a superstition that night air is injurious to health. Night air is the only kind of air there is at night, and fresh out-door air is far more whole-some than that which has been shut up in the house and breathed over and over again. Do not keep night air out; it is not a burglar. Since God has poured out an atmosphere of forty miles deep, all around the globe, it is a useless piece of economy to breath it more than once. An adult spoils one gallon of pure air every minute, or twenty-five flour barrels in a

ROAD TO HEALTH.

Up in the Morning Early.

HERE SHE GOES, THERE SHE GOES.

115

single night in breathing alone. Soiled or foul air can not purify any more than dirty water will clean dirty clothes. God's oxygen is the best tonic known.

Sunlight is second only in importance to fresh air. To convince one that light purifies air, it is only necessary to go into a darkened room and note the corrupt smell. A dark house is generally unwholesome and dirty. Where light is not permitted to enter, the physician will have to go. The sunlight will give a lady's cheeks a fresher tinge and more delicate complexion than all the French powders and rouge in Paris. Man makes houses but God made the out-doors with air and sunlight.

When passing from very cold air to the warmth of the house, go first to the coldest part of the house as the sudden transition from cold to hot air is very hurtful.

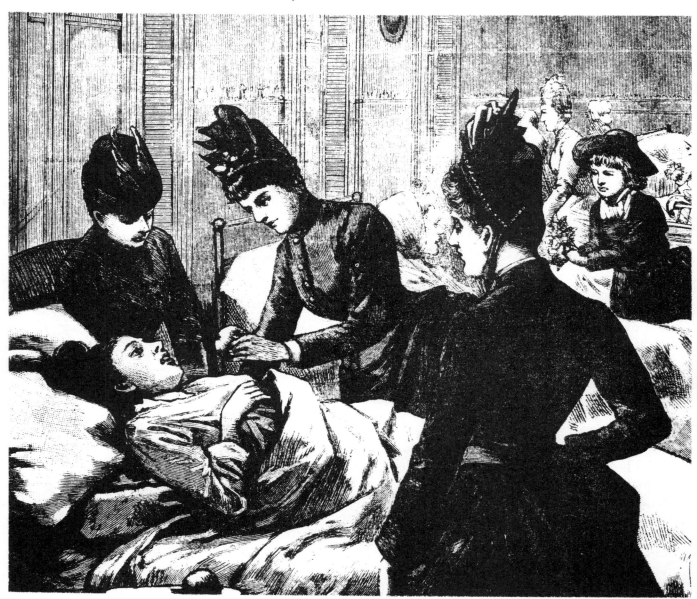

Pimples and Blotches Are Caused by Late Suppers

For sunburn and tan, wash the face before retiring with buttermilk or lemon juice.

Pimples and blotches are caused by late suppers, over-eating at meals, eating between meals, the use of candies, sweet-meats, preserves, and so on.

To prevent getting cold in cold weather, fold a newspaper and spread it across the chest. Persons having weak lungs can in this way make for them-selves a very cheap and perfect lung protector.

Many people who brush their teeth regularly and have a finely preserved set, use nothing but water. There is not a living soul who has to be told when he has a tooth-ache so no symptoms need to be given. Treat by applying a hot salt bag to the face, or a fig or raisin poultice made by boiling them in milk until they swell in size and place it between the gum and cheek. When a tooth is so far gone as to be very troublesome, it is best to have it out. Grasp it firmly as close to the gum as possible, with a small pair of pliers, give a rotatory motion with a strong and steady hand, and draw it out.

If you have stepped on a nail, bind a piece of the rind of salt pork on the part and keep quiet until it heals.

A Wet Shirt Will Cure Most Anything

A good way to harden the constitution is a bare-footed promenade on wet stones, newly fallen snow or grass. The grass is at its best when wet or covered with early morning dew.

Water cures tend to remove the roots of disease. First a hot, followed by a cold bath should be taken. Also, gushing with water, not a splash but by using a hose or can of water to the ailing part of the body is the cure of the disease. There are head, knee, upper body, lower body, hip, arm, and other gushes. Only undress the part of the body that you wish to gush, as to stand about much with no clothes on, whether before or after gushes, is harmful in the highest degree.

For the decline, showing loss of strength and unhealthy appearance, little appetite and bad humor. The best remedy would be to, every other day, lay on a wet sheet and cover with wet sheets and then take a cold upper and knee-gush, you will be healthy and strong.

The putting on of a wet shirt dipped in salt water, (vinegar may be added), and then covering with a warm quilt, will cure most anything.

Oil of Angle-Worms

Walking in water up to the ankles is good, but wormseed cures stomach and bowel complaints if taken in the amount of twenty-five drops every morning and walking in water. Whoever is suffering from melancholy, let him take his little box of worm-wood powder instead of his snuff-box, and put a pinch of it into his first spoonful of soup. Travel-

ers who are troubled with indigestion and nausea should never forget to take with them, as a faithful companion, their little bottle of worm-wood tincture.

For stiff joints, oil made by tying up common angle-worms is excellent to apply to sinews drawn up by sprains or disease. A valuable liniment is, one ounce worm-wood to one pint alcohol. Or, bruise the green stalks of worm-wood, moistened with vinegar, and apply to the sprain. Good for man or beast.

Castor Oil Sandwich

Tapeworms are said to be removed by refraining from supper and breakfast, and, at eight o'clock, taking one-third part of two-hundred minced pumpkin seeds, the shells of which have been removed by hot water. At nine take another third; at ten, the remainder. Follow it at eleven with a strong dose of castor-oil. Disguise castor-oil by covering the necessary dose with lemon juice, coffee, brandy or whiskey, but the best way is to make a castor-oil sandwich. Pour a layer of castor-oil on a layer of orange juice and cover with another layer of orange juice.

To rid one-self of warts, make a little roll of spider's web, lay it on the wart, set it on fire, and let it burn down on the wart.

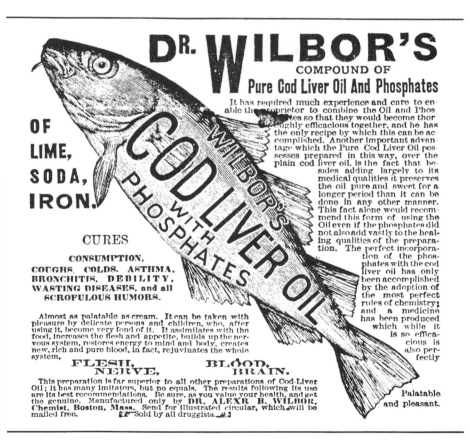

A dead man's hand will cure warts if rubbed upon them. However, if dead man's hands are scarce, a piece of meat can be used, then buried. As the meat decays the warts disappear. Stolen bacon also works.

The methods for removing warts are almost as numerous as the warts themselves. The best idea seems to be to tie a strong thread around it drawing it tighter each day.

Cultivate Jolly People and Bathe Daily

Leanness is caused by lack of power in the digestive organs to digest and assimilate the fat producing elements of food. First restore the digestion, take plenty of sleep, drink all the water the stomach will bear upon rising, take moderate exercise in open air, eat oatmeal, cracked wheat, graham mush, baked sweet apples, roasted and boiled beef, cultivate jolly people and bathe daily.

If you wish to be even more stout, or a trifle stouter, avoid excitement and keep your mind free from worry. Sit quietly for a long period and never make unnecessary movements. Eat all you can as often as you

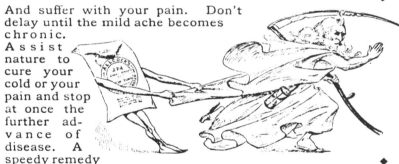

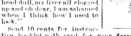

can, mostly of articles composed of starch, sugar and oil. Sleep as long as time allows and it won't be long before you will have that extra flesh on your frame and be known as a woman of ample proportions.

Corpulence occurs when anyone's constitution predisposes them to over feed. To reduce the excess, eat little or no butter, fat meat, gravies, sugar, vegetables or other articles containing large amounts of starch or sugar.

Dieting has sent many to the grave and will send many more due to ignorance. He omits one dinner and expects results; but by the time supper is ready, he feels as hungry as a dog, and eats like one, fast, furious and long.

Gather the blossoms of red clover when beginning to bloom, dry and put in a tight paper sack. A tea made from these blossoms is excellent for hives and cancer if patient will drink a gallon a day.

You who eat spiced salads at eleven o'clock must pay the penalty of outraged digestive organs. Eat nothing after six o'clock, retire at ten, sleep on your right side, keep window open five inches and other worlds will not disturb you much.

To overcome the appetite for liquor, or to cure the worst drunkard in the land, have him eat one orange one-half hour before breakfast. For intoxication apply cold water to the head, hot bricks to the feet and legs and make drink of the urine of a healthy person. This will quickly remove the intoxicating effects of liquor.

Head-aches

The serving of many and heavy wines at dinner is gradually becoming a thing of the past. Prominent men do not drink wines of any kind. A light wine and less assortment are the order of the day. Of course a dinner must have fluids, so now-adays mineral water is a good choice and many will call their hostesses blessed when they find it does not produce head-aches and kindred discomforts the following day.

For a head-ache, set a cloth in cold water, and lay it on the back of the neck. It will soothe the weary brain and quiet the nerves.

Migraine, is easy of cure. It proceeds from gases. It will be sufficient to wash the abdomen with cold water four times daily for three days. This complaint usually originates in disturbed circulation or some derangement of the stomach and bowels. The method will restore everything to order. "Be proud, a fool never gets migraine." Also, many have been relieved by chewing six to eight juniper-berries during the day.

Sick head-ache of females, exercise in the open air, even to fatigue. Earn an appetite. Avoid pickles, new bread and acids of all kinds.

For Consumption

This remedy for consumption is said to be an effectual one, and will, in time, completely cure the disorder: Live temperately, avoid spirituous liquors, wear flannel next to the skin, and every morning take half a pint of new milk mixed with a wine-glassful of the pressed juice of green hoarhound. This relieves the pains of the breast, gives ability to breathe deep, long and free, strengthens and harmonizes the voice and restores a better state of health.

Smaller than the Elbow

Nothing smaller than the elbow should be put in the ear. If deafness occurs examine if the cause be from insects. Apply a muslin bag filled with hops wrung out of hot water. In some cases, severe and long-continued deafness is treated with great success and efficiency by filling the mouth with the smoke of the strongest tobacco, instantly closing the mouth and nose, and then force the smoke through the nose but with holding the nostrils very tight. This forces the smoke through the eustachian tube into the ear. Repeat until one or both ears crack and the hearing returns. This method is simple, cheap and without hazard and therefore may be tried by anyone who chooses to do so.

ℐ ℐ ℰ ℰ

Move about good-naturedly; let your soul shine out as brightly as the sun at noon-day. It will warm yourself within, and all those whom you hold dear without. It will promote harmony of action in your physical machinery, and make all about you happy and more healthy.

Go to some intelligent man or woman and ask for a list of books that will be strengthening to your mental and moral condition. Life is short and your time for improvement so abbreviated, that you cannot afford to fill up with husks and cinders and debris.

Starched Collars Produce Short-sighted-ness

Never read in bed or when laying on the sofa. Sit with your back to the light, attend to your digestion, do not read longer than two hours without closing your eyes and resting them for five minutes. If your eyes are weak, bathe them in water to which a little salt and brandy have been added.

If you need to place an object nearer than 14 inches to your face to read, you need spectacles. No one under the age of forty should wear them as the accommodating power of the eyes has not been suspended.

Tight, starched collars can produce short-sighted-ness. The pressure of the collar upon the muscles of the neck disturb circulation. The fact most of us, if we live long enough, must come to wearing glasses makes it necessary to decide whether spectacles or eye glasses are better. From an aesthetic point of view, spectacles are preferred as more work can be done without fatigue. Still, for occasional use, folders, suspended by a light chain or cord are convenient. The young prefer pince-nez. Luckily the foibles of fashion have not foisted upon us the monocle or single

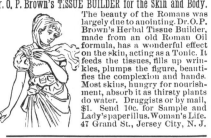

eye-glass, for it is use-less and ugly. Some people's eyes are so good that they do not fail to see things that are of no concern of theirs, their owners make them-selves a complete nuisance.

A Handkerchief over the Face

When some-one faints, do not get rattled. Place the patient flat on the back, loosen clothing, give plenty of air, sprinkle water on the face; give smelling salts to the nose, rub hands and feet and give brandy or whiskey. Keep the gathering crowd at least ten feet away. In case of injury, throw a handkerchief over the face to prevent the unpleasant sensation of the staring crowd.

When in the Sick-Room

By using the following recipe, you can be in a sick-room and not catch the disease. It was used during the plague and saved many lives. Wash the face and hands with it also: Take a large hand-ful each of rosemary, worm-wood, lavender, rue, sage and mint. Place in a stone jar, and turn over it one gallon of strong cider vinegar. Cover closely and keep near the fire for four days. Strain and add one ounce of pounded camphorgum. Bottle and keep tightly corked. Or, put a small lump of camphorgum, brinstone and assafetida in a little sock and tie around the body with a tape.

Never enter a room where a person is sick with an infectious disease if you have an empty stomach.

In disease, good nursing always plays a prominent part to recovery. The nurse must be intelligent, have goodness of heart, a kind and obliging disposition and good sense. In cases of the "very sick," watchers may be called in. Most night watchers are stupid, sleepy and ignorant of their duties; better to have a relative who will sleep in the same room.

Wear Flannel All Year

The best cold preventative is to wear scarlet-red flannel under-clothing on the chest all year and on the limbs in winter; never lean your back against anything cold.

To the strong and healthy, the flu is not dangerous but the weak or aged are often carried off by it.

An Excellent Soup for the Weakly

Put two cow-heels, and a breast of mutton into a large pan with four ounces of rice, one onion, 40 peppers, a turnip, a carrot and four gallons of water. Cover with brown paper and bake for six hours.

A bit of meat or pudding sent unexpectedly to a sick person often is the means of recalling long-lost appetite.

For cure of hypochondria, take a cold bath and ride horseback. Travel if you can afford it.

ℐ ℐ ℚ ℚ

A good way to cure rheumatism is to handle doves. Procure a number of them and stroke and play with them daily, and the result will be a cure, however, death to the doves. This proves that when one is afflicted with a malady so distressing and obstinate, one will resort to almost anything suggested.

ℐ ℐ ℚ ℚ

Twenty-five cents worth of Herrick's pills restores lost manhood, cures catarrh, cures one when it is such an effort to get up in the morning, cures liver complaint, and ministers to sore throat or loss of voice, and strenghtens the organs of speech. Soothes tortured nerves, lameness, blood disease and all disgusting and miserable ailments, and has saved many from an early grave.

ℐ ℐ ℚ ℚ

For blisters, bathe the feet in whiskey.

ℐ ℐ ℚ ℚ

Blowing in the ear will remove any foreign body located in the throat.

ℐ ℐ ℚ ℚ

Reading medical books sometimes frightens persons into the disease.

ℐ ℐ ℚ ℚ

Bind wild turnips around the feet to cure of corns. It won't take long, don't worry.

ℐ ℐ ℚ ℚ

To cure chilblains, soak feet for fifteen minutes in warm water, put on a pair of rubbers, without stockings, and go to bed.

In making of poultices, use bread, bran, charcoal, and mashed potatoes, free from lumps. Excellent in pneumonia, bronchitis, abscesses and boils. Mashed carrots are said to make a wound cleaner and healthier.

For Coughs and Colds

A poultice of garlic is good for most every-thing, although garlic makes one wink, drink and stink. Or a poultice of onions fried in lard and laid on the chest, or goose grease and molasses. Soak the feet in as hot water as can be bourne and drink a glass of hot lemonade. If all this

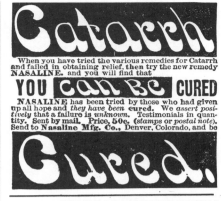

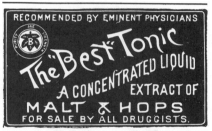

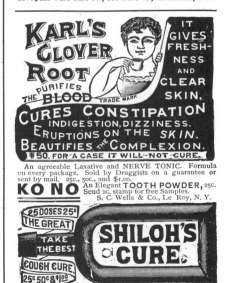

Madame Porter's
Cough Balsam,
Pleasant, Reliable, Effectual.
Successfully used for more than fifty years. Try it.

fails, try wrapping fat pork thick with pepper or a dirty woolen sock around the neck or fish skin tied to the feet.

Cough Medicine

1 pint Maltine
10 cents worth good brandy
10 cents worth glycerine

6 lemon, juice of
6 table-spoons sugar

Boil fifteen minutes and strain. This is a "sure-cure" for a cold in the head: As soon as you feel that you have a cold in the head, put a tea-spoonful of sugar in a goblet, and on it put six drops of camphor, fill the glass half full of water. Stir till the sugar is dissolved, then take a dessert-spoonful every twenty minutes.

For the lungs, a quart of tar, stirred six minutes in a gallon of water, and one-fourth taken four times a day, an hour or two after meals. It is said to clear the lungs and give greater ease in public speaking.

Go at the Usual Time and Solicit

Allow nothing short of fire or endangered life to induce you to resist, for one single moment, nature's call. Go at the usual time and solicit. In doing so you will have your reward in a degree of health-ful-ness and in length of life. Cold feet, sick headache, piles and scores of diseases, have their first foundations laid in constipation which is induced by resisting nature's first calls. Reader, let it be your wisdom never to do it again.

Helps for constipation are exercise, riding horseback, or to knead the belly and rub the bowels with hands, rubbing from left to right, take cool water and eat fruit. Use ice cold enemas and be quiet on a bed for treatment of diarrhea.

Constipation Remedy

Take one pound figs, one pound raisins, one pound dates, four ounces senna leaves.

Put all through a meat chopper and work the mixture into balls like small walnuts, keep in a tin box and take one at bedtime.

Rather than a bottle of hot water or a heated brick to warm the feet in bed, get some fine sand, dry it in a kettle on the stove, make a bag about eight inches square of flannel, fill with the dry sand, sew openings carefully together, cover the bag with a cotton cloth. Place on top of stove or in oven to heat. The sand will hold the heat a long time and is comfortable on the ailing person's hands or feet.

〆 〆 ℓ ℓ

To remove fish-bone from the throat, suck the juice of a lemon, and swallow it slowly. The citric acid never fails to dissolve the bone.

〆 〆 ℓ ℓ

Many children and men take cold after having their hair cut. This may be prevented by a quick dash of cold water on the head immediately after cutting, and before going out, and a brisk rubbing after-ward.

〆 〆 ℓ ℓ

A good cure for the croup is to take four or five holly-hock blossoms, boil and apply around the throat or dust a cloth thickly with nutmeg. Or, let a healthy person fill his lungs with pure air and slowly breathe upon the patient's throat and chest, commencing at the point of the chin and moving to the bottom of the wind-pipe.

〆 〆 ℓ ℓ

To prevent wearing through the skin when bed-ridden, apply to tender parts of the body with a feather, a mixture made by heating to a strong froth, the white of an egg, dropping in while beating two tea-spoonsful spirits of wine. Bottle for use.

For night sweats, put one or more basins of water under the bed of the patient, and renew every day. Or, have a strong healthy person occupy the bed with the patient for a few nights.

〆 〆 ℓ ℓ

Vomiting may be caused by riding back-wards in a carriage, rock-ing, waltzing or sailing in a vessel. This ailment is called motion sickness. Make a pad of wool or horse-hair and bind over the stomach. Lie down in open air and take brandy, spirits or raw salt oysters.

〆 〆 ℓ ℓ

The spider's-web is highly beneficial when applied to irritable sores also it gives a tranquilizing effect.

At the Sight of Blood

It is well for one to get accustomed to the sight of blood. Many can-not control them-selves under such circumstances. It is a good practice to witness an operation occasionally, or to assist in dressing a wound for the purpose of schooling one-self.

To stop bleeding, apply wet tea-leaves, or scrapings of sole-leather to a fresh cut. Cob-webs or puff balls will stop it also, be certain they are not mixed with filth of any kind.

When leeches are necessary to draw blood, hold the leeches over the spot by placing a wine glass over them holding until they bite. If

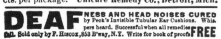
the leeches are held by hand, hold their tails with a wet cloth. If the leeches fail to bite, put first in cold water then moisten with sugar and water, cream, sweet beer, or prick ever so slightly, so as to draw blood. This will induce them to take. When they fall off full, put them on a plate and sprinkle salt all over them. If the leeches stick to the skin too long, never pull off but touch them with salt.

For the making of a mustard plaster for children, take one teaspoonful of mustard, three of wheat flour and water to the consistency of a stiff batter. Apply between soft muslin cloths. For adults take one part of mustard and two of flour.

And Keep the Bowels Open

Vapors or low spirits can be determined when the patient wears a melancholy expression and imagines he has some violent disease. May even hear imaginary noises. Do not laugh at or reason with. Be certain food is well masticated and there is daily exercise in the open air of riding, gunning or fishing.

Hysteria or hysterics is a peculiar affliction suffered by lively nervous females with vivid imaginations. This may be due to exciting books, tight lacing, luxurious living, theatrical exhibitions, disappointed love, grief, anger or fright. Snuff applied to the nostrils will sometimes relieve. Wash freely with cold water and keep the bowels free. Insanity should be cured in the hospital, but the most common cause is obstructed bowels.

However, it seems to be well noticed that most females never have hysterical fits when alone. It seems that some of our ladies make a noise for attention and fall to the ground without injury to her person or her dress.

Lightning sometimes kills innocent people, even sober, temperate men. When a person is struck by lightning, strip the body and throw buckets of cold water over it from ten to fifteen minutes; inflate the lungs and apply continual frictions all over the body; apply blisters to the breast, and administer stimulants; such as brandy.

If you find a person hanging, cut down the body without letting it fall. If the body is still warm, stand off six feet and dash several times with a bowl of cold water.

If your lower garments catch fire, do not run. Sit upon them. If upper clothing is on fire, throw a shawl or blanket around your body and lie down and roll, keeping your mouth closed or you will be burned internally.

Learn to Swim

Every one should learn to swim. No animal, fowl or reptile requires to be taught, and few persons exist who have not some time or other seen a bull-frog perform his masterly movements in the water. It would detract from no one's dignity to take a few lessons from him. Learn to swim, cost what it will. If there is an accident on the water, and you are unable to swim, draw the breath in well, keep the mouth tight shut, do not struggle and throw the arms up, but yield quietly to the water. Hold the head up and everything else under water. To prevent drowning, a felt or silk hat held so as to keep the crown full of air, will sustain a person above water for a great length of time.

To recover the body of a drowned person, supply yourself with some glass jars and a quantity of unslaked lime and go out in a boat to where the person was seen to go down. Fill one of the jars half full of lime and fill with water and tightly cork. Drop into the water and it will explode at the bottom of the river with a loud report. Do at least three times in a different place around the area and the body will raise to the surface.

Warm Feet Save Lives

The scuffing of the feet in thin-soled slippers over woollen carpet will warm cold feet until they are burning hot. Incomparably better than fire warmth or hot water.

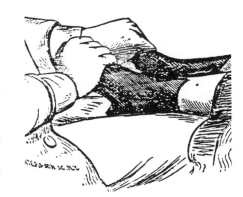

There is no such thing as a record of those who die annually from cold feet, but warm feet would have cured many of them. The best suggestion, and you'll bless me for this, is to have some kind friend hold your feet in his or her hands, for about twenty minutes every evening. The shoes must remain on. Place the feet in the lap of your friend; thumbs and fingers should grasp the toes of the shoes firmly. Apply pressure and it will impart magnetic warmth. One of the opposite sex is preferable, and not a husband or wife, as the magnetic forces are stronger with those less familiar.

Anyone Still Alive around Age 100
Soon Dies from the Inability to Live

Ten days per annum is the average sickness of human life. Till 50 it is but half, and after 50 it rapidly increases. The mixed and fanciful diet of man is the cause of numerous diseases from which animals are exempt. At age 50 man's appetite fails, complexion fades, and the tongue is apt to be furred on the least exertion of body or mind. Muscles become flabby, joints weak, spririts droop and sleep is imperfect and unrefreshing. After 80 years of age life is rather endurance than enjoyment. The nerves are blunted, the senses fail, the muscles are rigid, the tubes become hard, the memory fails, the brain ossifies, the affections are buried, and hope ceases. Anyone still alive around age 100 soon dies from the inability to live.

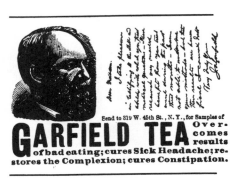

God's Rule of Health

Simple food, mostly of vegetables, fish and fowl.
Plenty of sleep, with very early hours for retiring.
Flannel clothing next to the skin all the year round;
Feet kept warm, head cool, and nothing worn tight.
Just as much exercise as possible, only let fresh air and sunshine go
   together.
No tea or coffee for the children, no alcoholic drink or tobacco for
   anybody.
Tell the truth and mind your parents.

   If everyone obeyed these rules they'd have a happy, well-to-do life
as our Heavenly Father has made it for us in the world, if we will only
take hold of it by the right handle.

For Bilious and Nervous Disorders, such as Wind and Pain in the Stomach, Sick Headache, Giddiness, Fulness, and Swelling after Meals, Dizziness and Drowsiness, Cold Chills, Flushings of Heat, Loss of Appetite, Shortness of Breath, Costiveness, Scurvy, Blotches on the Skin, Disturbed Sleep, Frightful Dreams, and all Nervous and Trembling Sensations, &c. THE FIRST DOSE WILL GIVE RELIEF IN TWENTY MINUTES. This is no fiction. Every sufferer is earnestly invited to try one Box of these Pills, and they will be acknowledged to be a Wonderful Medicine.—"Worth a guinea a box."
   BEECHAM'S PILLS, taken as directed, will quickly restore females to complete health. For a

WEAK STOMACH, IMPAIRED DIGESTION, DISORDERED LIVER,

they ACT LIKE MAGIC:—a few doses will work wonders upon the Vital Organs; Strengthening the muscular System; restoring long-lost Complexion; bringing back the keen edge of appetite, and arousing with the ROSEBUD OF HEALTH the whole physical energy of the human frame. These are "facts" admitted by thousands, in all classes of society, and one of the best guarantees to the Nervous and Debilitated is that BEECHAM'S PILLS HAVE THE LARGEST SALE OF ANY PATENT MEDICINE IN THE WORLD. Full directions with each box.
   Prepared only by THOS. BEECHAM, St. Helens, Lancashire, England.
Sold by Druggists generally. B. F. ALLEN & CO., 365 and 367 Canal St., New York, Sole Agents for the United States, who, if your druggist does not keep them (inquire first),
WILL MAIL BEECHAM'S PILLS ON RECEIPT OF PRICE, 25 CENTS A BOX.
   Mention this publication.

Dust to Dust

The aged need amusement, but it should be of a quiet, unexciting nature. Read to them, listen to them. One of the greatest pleasures of old age consists of old memories and associations.

Now the excesses committed earlier in life are told. Now we have to watch what we eat, the air we breathe and the exercise we take. We must keep clean and nice and warm. The simpler we live the longer is our stay in the world.

The age women begin to exhibit signs of infirmity and decrepitude, and when diseases come into play, is usually around the fifty-third year. With men it is the sixtieth year.

When caring for the sick, never speak in low tones or whisper as the patient can not fully understand, and this causes needless apprehension.

Some patients can not bear any noise, even the rustle of a silk dress or shoes that creak.

Patients are often killed by kindness, a spoonful of improper food or indulgence of some whim. Many a tombstone might be inscribed, "talked to death by well-meaning friends."

Disease always sends a warning cry ahead. If heeded, illness will be averted and death prevented. In the last stage of an incurable disease the face becomes what nurses call "struck with death." The forehead becomes wrinkled and dry, the eyes sunken, the nose pointed and bordered with a dark or violet circle; the temples sunken, hollow and retired; the ears sticking up, the lips hanging down, the cheeks sunken, the chin

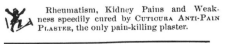

wrinkled and hard, the colour of the skin leaden or violet; the hair of the nose and eyelashes sprinkled with yellowish white dust.

Before it is too late it is best to remember that "Nobody ever went to sleep indifferent to religion and waked up in Heaven."

As soon as the patient has stopped breathing, straighten the limbs and place the arms by the side or across the chest as desired. Close the eye-lids and keep them closed with your fingers or by placing something, such as a penny upon them.

False teeth should be placed in the mouth soon, before the jaws have set. Close the mouth and tie a handkerchief from under the jaw to the top of the head, tight enough to make the mouth closed and look natural. Comb hair, and if a woman, braid the hair. Wash and dress the body, however, if the body is clean it is a needless exposure and unnecessary annoyance to wash it. Tie the knees and ankles together.

A Black Ribbon Fastened to the Door-Bell

The fact that a death has occurred should be made known to the outer world immediately by closing all blinds, or drawing the long linen shades. A black ribbon should be fastened to the door-bell. From this moment until the funeral cortege leaves for the church or cemetery, none of the feminine members can be seen. Dress-makers can be persuaded to call at the house to give fittings for suitable mourning dress. The mourning dress for a widow consists of a black worsted skirt and waist, trimmed very simply with folds or English crepe, a bonnet made wholly of crepe, with a long crepe veil falling in the rear to the knees, or even lower, and for the first month an equally long veil falling over the face. Elderly ladies are in mourning for one and one-half to two years, widow's for two years. However, many ladies of unquestionable taste and discretion now content themselves simply with wearing clothes that are black in colour. Ladies must not be present at a burial.

When Not Certain of Death

If you are not certain of death, keep the body until signs of decay are seen before you allow an under-taker to come. Not many people have been buried alive—but some have.

The process of death is the reverse process of development. When life ceases to show improvement and happiness it is of no value. Those who live longest are those who accomplish the most good. For the aged that have lived life to the fullest, usefully and joyfully, a natural death is welcome as it is most beautiful. The soul is triumphant, serene, and happy. There is now a new found freedom and higher and brighter sphere of existence.

Who Wants to Live Forever?

It might be a bright day when you push off from this planet, or it may be on a dark night, while the owl is hooting from the forest. The apple orchards may be in full bloom or the earth shrouded with snow. I know not the time, I know not the mode; but the days of life are being subtracted away until the breath will fail, the eyes close, the heart stopped, the tongue still—all still. But this ought not to be a depressing theme; die we must, who wants to live forever?

Bibliography

Aster, Jane. *The Habits of Good Society,* Rudd & Company, New York, New York, 1860.

Ayres, Alfred. *The Mentor,* D. Appleton & Company, 1902.

Child, Lydia Maria. *The Frugal Housewife,* Marsh & Capen, Boston, Massachusetts, 1829.

Cooper, Thomas, M.D. *A Treatise of Domestic Medicine,* George Getz, Reading, Pennsylvania, 1824.

Corson, Miss Juliet. *Miss Corson's Practical American Cookery and Household Management,* Dodd, Mead & Company, New York, New York, 1886.

Fillippini, Alessandro. *The Table,* Charles L. Webster & Company, New York, New York, 1890.

Foote, Edward B., M.D. *Dr. Foote's Plain Home Talk Embracing Medical Common Sense,* Murray Hill Publishing Company, New York, New York, 1891.

Fowler, L. N. *Fowler on Marriage,* Fowler & Wells, New York, New York, 1853.

Hazlitt, W. Carew. *Old Cookery Books,* Elliot Stock, London, England, 1886.

Herrick, Dr. *The American Domestic Cook-Book,* G. Benthuysen & Sons, Albany, New York, 1867.

Holt, Emily. *Encyclopedia of Etiquette,* Page and Company, 1916.

Howard, Horton. *An Improved System of Botanic Medicine*, Published by Author, Columbus, Ohio, 1833.

Humphrey, Frederick, M.D. *Humphrey's Mentor & Medical Advisor,* Humphrey's Homeo Medicine Company, New York, New York, (19th century).

Jewry, Mary. *Warne's Model Cookery and Housekeeping Book,* Frederick Warne & Company, London, England, 1868.

Kirkpatrick, Mrs. T. J. *The Modern Cook Book and Practical Suggestions,* Corwell & Kirkpatrick, Springfield, Ohio, 1890.

Kneipp, Rev. Sabastian. *The Kneipp Cure*, The Kneipp Cure Publishing Company, New York, New York, 1892.

Morse, Sidney Levi & Isabel Gordon Curtis. *Household Discoveries & Mrs. Curtis's Cook Book,* The Success Company, Petersburg, New York, 1914.

Oliver, Dr. N. T. *Lee's Priceless Recipes,* Laird & Lee, Chicago, Illinois, 1895.

Parloa, Maria. *Home Economics*, The Century Company, New York, New York, 1910.

Parloa, Maria. *Miss Parloa's New Cook Book*, Etses & Lauriat, Boston, Massachusetts, 1880.

Ritter, T. J. & Alice Gitchell Kirk. *The People's Home Library,* R. C. Barum Company, Toronto, Canada, and Imperial Publishing Company, Cleveland, Ohio, 1915.

Sloan, Dr. Earl S. *Sloan's Handy Hints and Up-To-Date Cook Book,* Boston, Massachusetts, 1901.

Trall, Russell T. *Hydropathic Cook-Book*, Fowlers & Wells, New York, New York, 1854.

Willard, Frances E. *Glimpses of Fifty Years,* H. J. Smith & Company, Chicago, Illinois, 1889.

Williams, Mary E. *Elements of the Theory and Practice of Cookery,* The MacMillan Company, London, England, 1901.

Buckeye Cookery, Buckeye Publishing Company, Minneapolis, Minnesota, 1877.

Confer's Year Book and Almanac, The S. D. Confer Medical Company, Orangeville, North Dakota, 1906.

Conklins Handy Manual of Useful Information & Atlas of the World, 19th century.

The Cottage Physician, King-Richardson Publishing Company, 1896.

Harper's Bazar, Harper & Brothers, New York, New York, 1888-1893.

The Home Messenger Book of Tested Receipts, For the Detroit Home of the Friendless & The Thompson Home for Old Ladies, E. B. Smith & Company, Detroit, Michigan, 1873.

The Household Treasure, Barclay & Company, Philadelphia, Pennsylvania, 1864.

The Ladies Home Journal, Curtis Publishing Company, Philadelphia, Pennsylvania, 1889-1895.

The National Encyclopaedia of Business & Social Forms, The National Publishing Company, Philadelphia, Pennsylvania, 1879.

The Manners That Win, Buckeye Publishing Company, Minneapolis, Minnesota, 1882.

The New Buckeye Cook Book & Practical Housekeeping, Webb Publishing, St. Paul, Minnesota, 1905.

Our Chefs Best Receipts, Rand & McNally & Company, Chicago and New York, 1899.

Mrs. Owens' Cook Book and Useful Household Hints, J. M. Ball, Little Rock, Arkansas, 1886.

Illustrations

Cirker, Blanche. *1800 Woodcuts by Thomas Bewick and His School,* Dover Publications, New York.

Hart, Harold H. Picture Archives, *Humor, Wit & Fantasy; Trades & Professions; Dining & Drinking; Goods & Merchandise,* Hart Publishing Company, New York.

Harter, Jim. *Women; Men,* Dover Publications, New York.

Rowe, William. *Goods & Merchandise,* Dover Publications, New York.

Harper's Bazar, Harper & Brothers, New York, 1888-1893.

Old Engravings & Illustrations, The Dick Sutphen Studio, Minneapolis, Minnesota.

The Ladies Home Journal, Curtis Publishing Company, Philadelphia, Pennsylvania, 1889-1895.

Barbara Fairchild Gramm lives in St. Paul with her husband Milt (their picture is on the back cover). She has worked for the Burlington Northern Railroad for the past 29 years.

Barb is grateful to her parents, Arnold & Myrtle Fairchild, for deciding to bring her into the world instead of building a fireplace.

She loves being "Mom" to David St. Martin of St. Paul; Steve & his wife Nancy St. Martin of Maplewood; and, Suzanne & her husband Gino Rodriguez of Eagan.

Being "Gramma" to Matthew Steven St. Martin & Nicole Marie Rodriguez makes Barb HAPPY! The entire family is eagerly anticipating three more babies presently in the oven.